The Process of Becoming a Counsellor

This book aims to help the reader understand what is involved in becoming a counsellor, and what to expect of the experience of counsellor training.

Covering everything from interviewing for practitioner training, doing personal and professional development, to seeing your very first client, this book gives a thorough, step-by-step examination of the process of becoming a counsellor. It draws upon the authors' diverse experience of working within the counselling field, academic research and personal testimonies from a wide range of counselling students. Readers will gain valuable insight into the personal demands/responsibilities and the transformation that training and qualifying involves. Included throughout the book are pedagogical features such as reflection points, vignettes, case studies, and activities which will help prepare readers for the experiential process they will go through.

The Process of Becoming a Counsellor is an important resource for anyone planning to start or just beginning counselling training. It is a must-read for anyone contemplating a counselling qualification or who may be wondering if training to be a counsellor is the right pathway for them.

Jayne Godward is a Person-Centred counsellor and supervisor who has been teaching counselling skills and counselling since 1993 and has taught on counselling practitioner courses in FE colleges and Universities since 2006. Jayne is the director of Yorkshire Counselling Training working with students on the introductory courses, CPCAB L3 Certificate, L4 Diploma and L6 Certificate in Supervision.

Tara Fox is a BACP accredited relational psychotherapist and clinical supervisor. She is a senior lecturer in integrative counselling and mental health at Leeds Beckett University. She has worked in education since 1999 delivering counselling training and personal development courses in community, FE and HE environments from introduction to Masters level.

"This book is a must-read for anyone considering or currently in counselling training. Comprehensive and accessible, it offers a clear guide to selecting the right course, navigating the application process, and understanding key aspects of training such as supervision, personal therapy, and experiential groups. The book offers valuable insights into the benefits and challenges of self-awareness, the role of personal reflection, and the unconscious motivations for pursuing therapy. It thoughtfully addresses important topics such as diversity and the challenges of working in a rapidly changing global environment. This is an indispensable resource for aspiring therapists."

Clare Camm, Senior Lecturer in Integrative Psychotherapy, Metanoia Institute, BACP Accredited Counsellor and Psychotherapist, UK

"This is a must have book for potential counselling course trainees. Jayne and Tara have put together an excellent book exploring the personal impact and professional learning on counselling training courses. They have generously shared some of their own personal stories and new professional struggles when they completed counselling training. I highly recommend this book and I wish that I had a copy of it at the beginning of my training."

John Bradley, Counsellor, Supervisor and Trainer in Private Practice (Hull and York) Former trainer at the Ellesmere Centre in Hull; BACP Senior Accredited Counsellor and Supervisor, UK

"This book provides a comprehensive and yet highly accessible companion to those considering therapeutic training. This book captures the challenges and learning curves on the personal and professional journey undertaken by trainees from consideration of the range of different therapeutic approaches and selection of a programme of study to securing a practice placement. This book examines and highlights the developmental stages experienced by the trainee therapist and covers the wide range of questions and answers that any would-be therapist might need to consider before embarking on a programme of study. In conclusion, this book is an invaluable resource for anyone considering therapy training."

Bo Bloomfield, relational therapist and EMDR practitioner working in schools, colleges and university as well as in private practice, College Counselling Placement Manager, MBACP (Senior Accredited) Counsellor and Clinical Supervisor, Certified Clinical Trauma Professional (CCTP-I and CCTPII), UK

The Process of Becoming a Counsellor

Navigating the Transformation

Jayne Godward and Tara Fox

Routledge
Taylor & Francis Group

NEW YORK AND LONDON

Designed cover image: Getty

First published 2026
by Routledge
605 Third Avenue, New York, NY 10158

and by Routledge
4 Park Square, Milton Park, Abingdon, Oxon OX14 4RN

Routledge is an imprint of the Taylor & Francis Group, an informa business

Library of Congress Cataloging-in-Publication Data
A catalog record for this title has been requested

ISBN: 978-1-032-52248-7 (hbk)
ISBN: 978-1-032-52249-4 (pbk)
ISBN: 978-1-003-40575-7 (ebk)

DOI: 10.4324/9781003405757

Typeset in Times New Roman
by Taylor & Francis Books

Contents

Figures

Boxes

Acknowledgements

A big thank you to all our past and present students, supervisees and colleagues who have contributed their personal accounts and experiences to this book.

To my dear partner, Mark who has supported and encouraged me to finish this project. - Jayne Godward

Gratitude to all who have given generously to this endeavour. Huge appreciation and love to my partner, Andy, and son Conner for their emotional support, and to my daughter Maia for her artwork contributions. - Tara Fox

Preface: How this book came about

Since 2012 I have been the business partner and lead tutor of a private training organisation which offers pathways in counselling from introduction to practitioner level. Over the years I have dealt with many enquiries from people who wanted to become counsellors but were not aware of what was involved, particularly the personal demands of embarking on this training. Often people wanted a fast track to a very responsible profession or thought they could just go and 'do unto' someone else not realising the personal investment and personal work which would be required.

The idea for this book came as I felt that there was a need for an accessible and comprehensive guide as to what is involved using the real experiences of trainees.

As I discussed the plan for the book with Tara, we began to have a real interest in capturing the process which students go through, having witnessed the development of different people over our joint 40+ years of being involved with counsellor training.

As we discussed the format of the book, we set an aim to examine the different aspects of the process of transformation and what we called the 'shift' from being a 'lay person' to a qualified practitioner who has the self-understanding and self-awareness to work competently and ethically with vulnerable clients.

This has led us down some interesting avenues and we have learned a lot through this endeavour which has informed our practice as tutors, and we hope our readers will find this text both interesting and enlightening.

I think this book encapsulates the process of becoming a counsellor which we have witnessed and heard about first hand from our students.

Jayne Godward
2025

Introduction

Jayne Godward and Tara Fox

The aim of this book

The aim of this book is to help you to understand what is involved in becoming a counsellor or therapist. It is important to understand the process that a prospective trainee will normally go through to be competent to work as a counsellor and to be able to support and empower the vulnerable clients they are going to encounter. The aim is to help you think about the aspects involved which may not be obvious to you as a lay person.

This is also aimed at people who are unsure or wondering if training to be a counsellor or psychotherapist is the right pathway for them. We are presuming that the reader has very little knowledge of the experience of this transformational process. It will be particularly relevant for those studying introductory counselling courses or those on learning programmes at pre- practitioner level, who are thinking about the next step.

Aspects of the book will be helpful for those on Year 1 of a therapist training course at undergraduate or post-graduate level, who are about to start placement, supervision and personal therapy to help them prepare mentally for this process. Tutors may also find this book useful as a guide to students as it answers some of the questions learners need to know during their training.

In this book you will find out about student and tutor experiences of the different aspects of training and will be informed as to what to expect. In a way it gives a warning as to the pitfalls and challenges of taking on this professional training with its personal demands which are very different from other professional courses.

Looking inside the book

This book will cover the process of becoming a counsellor or psychotherapist. It is less about practical advice but more about preparing you for what you can expect in terms of the experience of doing counsellor or psychotherapy training.

DOI: 10.4324/9781003405757-1

Although the term 'counsellor' will be used often, we will also use the term therapist as these two terms are used interchangeably in the counselling and psychotherapy courses we have taught on.

We refer at times to the 'BACP' which stands for the British Association for Counselling and Psychotherapy. This is the largest UK counselling and therapy body and the organisation which both Tara and Jayne belong to.

We also refer to 'pre-practitioner' courses which may be undergraduate or post-graduate certificate courses which develop skills and knowledge but do need lead to a counsellor or therapist qualification or involve a professional practice element.

There is some factual information about aspects of training (Chapter 1) and the models of counselling (Chapter 7), but the book's main focus is on the process a person will go through if they embark on this personal and professional journey. We start at the beginning with why a person would want to become a counsellor as we feel it is important to look at underlying motives (Chapter 2) and go on to look at the personal challenges to self (Chapter 4) and aspects of identity and diversity (Chapter 5) and the possible impact on self and others from doing this training. (Chapter 6). There is also a chapter on the selection process which, will help you to prepare for an application to a course programme (see Chapter 3).

The experience of developing as a person and actually becoming a therapist is examined using some personal accounts from students (Chapters 8, 9 and 10) then we look at the actual first client experience (Chapter 11) and what this means to actually counsel and the demands of taking on this role. The impacts of societal and global issues are included at this stage as these cannot be excluded from the counselling training and client work (Chapter 12).

The final part of the book looks at how the trainee can and is required to support themselves with chapters on self-care, supervision and personal therapy. The value of these methods of personal and professional support are examined.

We wanted to make the book student-friendly and have included learner features like ponder or reflection points, case studies and activities in most chapters to enable you to reflect on the topics being covered in relation to yourselves. We have included personal experiences and anecdotes from past and current students, tutors and placement providers to help make the subject matter of chapters more interesting and accessible. At times we share our own experiences as we have gone through this process ourselves and continue to teach on training programmes. We will be drawing on current research into the areas covered by the book, mainly in the UK but also from international research. We have also undertaken our own research into some areas which have not been formally covered before so we hope these will be of some interest to the reader.

Chapter 1

The training process

Tara Fox

Introduction

This chapter speaks transparently about the design of counselling programmes helping you to see the rationale behind the way courses are typically run from the introductory level to the qualifying practitioner courses, e.g., undergraduate (UG) or post-graduate (PG) Diploma or masters (MA). The different training and assessment components for the various levels are explained including how these link directly to becoming a counsellor who is a reflective professional practitioner.

The training experience is often surprising because the focus is on what you think and feel as much as the practice of skills or reading and understanding of theories. For some this is great news because you get the chance to speak about your life experiences and emotions, for others this makes the courses harder to participate in.

In this chapter I will help you understand:

- the definitions of counselling and psychotherapy
- an overview of the training process including the typical course training components for different levels and the assessment expectations of the different course levels
- how learning is facilitated by the counselling tutor.

Defining counselling and psychotherapy

Counselling can be described as an umbrella term covering a range of talking therapies that are all interpersonal therapeutic relationships. The frustrating fact that there is no single universal definition arises from the way definitions depend on the view of the approach to counselling and there are many different approaches. In fact, recent research tells us there could be as many as 500 types of therapy out there (Prochaska and Norcross, 2018).

Organisations use the role of 'counsellor' to mean advice, guidance and helping services too which further adds to the confusion for anyone learning

DOI: 10.4324/9781003405757-2

about it. Debt counsellors for example are not therapeutic but are great at giving practical support and advice. Counsellors on the other hand are qualified clinical healthcare professionals.

The Oxford English Dictionary defines counselling as:

> a form of therapy assisting people to deal effectively with emotional or psychological issues through talking with a professional counsellor.
>
> (OED, 2025)

The largest professional body in the UK, the British Association of Counselling and Psychotherapy define counselling as:

> Counselling and psychotherapy are umbrella terms that cover a range of talking therapies. They are delivered by trained practitioners who work with people over a short or long term to help them bring about effective change and/or enhance their wellbeing.
>
> (BACP, 2021)

There is continued debate as to the difference between counselling and psychotherapy with the British Association for Counselling and Psychotherapy (BACP) pointing out how counsellor and psychotherapist terms are used 'interchangeably' meaning either or can be used to describe the role. For example, I am a BACP accredited counsellor, and the status means I may call myself a counsellor or psychotherapist. The etymology of the latter word is fascinating to me as it comes from the Greek *psyche* (soul) and *therapeia* (serve) meaning servant of the soul.

In the UK the UK Council for Psychotherapy (UKCP) define psychotherapy as follows

> Sometimes 'psychotherapy' and 'psychotherapeutic counselling,' are called 'talking therapies.' For the most part, this is because they involve talking about an emotional difficulty with a trained therapist. That might be anything from grief to anxiety, relationship difficulties to addiction.
>
> (UKCP, 2025)

The standards set by the UKCP place this role apart from counselling training and the job market, especially in the NHS, which pays a much higher rate for UKCP trained psychotherapists who typically study at postgraduate level and are required to undertake many more hours of personal therapy often bi-weekly. The pay scales for these roles in the NHS are higher than counsellors and therefore the hierarchy exists between counselling and psychotherapy much to the frustration of counsellors who wish to keep their psychotherapy title and associated prestige.

In America counsellors are required to study at master's level to achieve the title of 'counselor' and licence to practice. They have the title of 'mental health counselor' and more commonly across states 'licensed professional counselor' but they use the term psychotherapy to mean the work of the counsellor (ACA, n.d.).

In the UK the BACP are trying to address where counselling ends and psychotherapy begins through their Scope of Practice and Education for the counselling and psychotherapy professions (SCoPEd). Its aim is to agree a common, 'evidence-based competence framework' (BACP, 2022).

To respect how counsellors and psychotherapists work I will use the terms interchangeably recognising how competent both of these roles are and that these competency scales have many cross overs.

Overview of the training process

Counselling training courses are designed specifically to develop three aspects namely practical counselling skills which are sometimes called 'interventions' as they are practised for a purpose, to help your 'client,' theory because counselling involves a good deal more than just listening and finally, but arguably the most important aspect, personal development.

Most students will study at college or in community settings beginning with an introductory/Level 2 course that introduces them to the skills one by one with an opportunity to observe, practise and reflect on experience.

Theory at this level is basic but you will still need to show an understanding of the skills and underlying theory through writing about them. Courses at these levels are often portfolio-based and you are supported to meet learning criteria through guided discussion, activities, practical sessions, and observations from peers and your tutor. Consequently, you will have a sense of achievement knowing you are literally ticking off the demands of the course along the way.

Sometimes people become interested in counselling courses because of their local availability. I have taught many professionals in community settings who enjoy dipping their foot in the water before investing further in the qualifying courses. Some at this point decide to shift course from community/college setting to the university environment. Local courses are a good way of working out if you want to study further in the pathway and for some the achievement at the introductory level adds value to their existing role leading to further promotion at work. For example:

> My work as a nurse has developed more into the need for mental health support. I trained in counselling skills at my local community centre and achieved the level 2 qualification. I was then Ok to apply for a new role at work where I could make good use of the skills I had learnt. I did not want to leave my nursing job so this was ideal.

The progression course following on from level 2 is normally the level 3 and this prepares you for practitioner training at level 4 (Diploma). Some students who already have a degree in a different subject swap to a university setting after level 2 to progress their counselling training pathway to do a PG certificate followed by the PG Diploma.

Assessment at level 3 will require a portfolio of evidence that shows you have met a range of criteria, and you need to be organised and tick off your progress along the way. Courses will cover your practical skills competency, your self-awareness and your knowledge of the theories (psychological theory). There is a good deal of theory to learn at level 3 some of which is tested through an exam. Some from an essay that includes a comparison of approaches so that you can consider alternative options. On level 3 courses I have, for example, taught the person-centred approach as the main modality, then offered the key concepts of CBT and psychodynamic approach. This helps students to see the similarities and differences of theories and how these offer a perspective on client issues and therefore influence and impact on the interventions used in practice.

No placement is required but weekly skills practice helps you to feel more natural in the role. You generally shift from *conscious incompetence*, i.e., you know what you can't do to *conscious competence*, i.e., you know what you can do to *unconscious competence*, where the skills are integrated into your repertoire of responses.

Interestingly as counselling educators we are required to make our unconscious competence conscious and aim to explain processes as simply as possible. There will normally be a case study as part of the assessment where you can show knowledge of ethical working with a student client on your course over three consecutive counselling sessions. This is set up to be supported through a supervision group experience too and simulates a professional process for real case work.

After this, students who do not have a degree may apply for the Diploma in Counselling (level 4) or swap to a university setting to study a HE Diploma to become a qualified counsellor.

Some people choose a Level 4 Diploma route even if they already have a degree like this example here:

> I wanted a change from social work so I chose to study at a community centre where I could enjoy discussing theories and philosophies, share my experiences, and learn from others in a smaller setting. Here I felt free to be brave and try out new skills, be honest about my insecurities and we soon bonded. It was the best learning experience I have ever had. and to this day we still meet as a group from time to time. I think because I already had a degree, I did not feel the need to prove my academic skills, and I found it helpful to tick off my progress every week keeping my portfolio of evidence.

If you have a degree and would like to advance your academic qualifications, then you can learn more about counselling through the study of a PG Certificate (level 7). This will give you the solid training in counselling skills and theory to be able to develop in your existing job role and prepares you for practitioner level training.

I lead a PG certificate course where GPs, Social workers and nurses for example wish to increase their skills to enhance their current job role. Others discover they have found the right path and progress to the practitioner-level courses like the PG Diploma/MA in counselling.

Post Graduate Certificate level training covers essential theory, ethics, skills competency and personal development. There are likely to be lectures about theory, practice of skills sessions and personal time for reflection on your experiences. These will lead up to a practical assessment of your ability to utilise counselling skills in a timed session (usually 10 mins), a written reflection on that performance which could be a transcript and/ or analysis of the session. There is normally a theory essay to assess your theoretical knowledge of the counselling approach(es) where you will evaluate and present an academic discussion of these ideas, considering different evidence and opinions. Finally, you will normally keep a journal or do a reflective written assignment focusing on your self-awareness and growth arising from being on the course. A typical learning outcome for a PG Cert theory module is: 'Critically discuss a range of psychological theories related to counselling.'

A student said:

> I was asked to choose a mental health issue and to critically analyse different approaches to helping that issue. I chose social anxiety and learnt a lot about how CBT and Transactional approaches can both offer effective ways to understand and manage this.

Practitioner level training Diploma, PG Diploma or MA

Practitioner training requires a placement where you log every counselling hour to build up to the full amount needed (usually 100), a supervisor for this work (from an approved list) who you will need to see at least once a month sometimes every two weeks for the time you are on placement. You often need to see a counsellor too for a number of hours to scaffold you through the personal development aspect. This varies from ten hours upwards depending on the organisation or professional body. The theories are more in-depth and you are encouraged to self-reflect on the personal meanings of these theories in your own life.

Practitioner courses have more emphasis on professional practice issues such as ethical dilemmas and assessment issues, along with increased focus on personal and professional development and self-reflection to prepare you for working with clients. Personal development becomes more important because

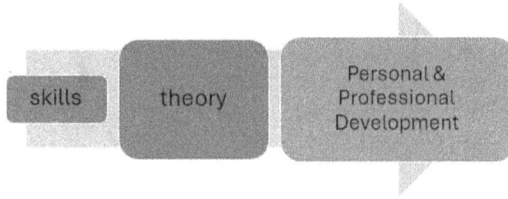

Figure 1.1

effective counselling depends on the quality of the relationship (Norcross, 2002; Elkins, 2016) and this means you will need to tune into the needs of your client as an individual and adjust your responses appropriately. An example might be where your client speaks using a lot of metaphors and so you may need to connect through this medium by joining in with this creative type of communication. This requires reflection in action during the moment and on action after the event (Schön, 1983) with an intention to understand the meaning of each interaction in the sessions.

You are developing into a reflective practitioner and as such will need to keep a reflective learning log/journal of some kind.

The journal

This is normally kept private to you but gives you a sensible place to make observations about yourself and how others may be impacting on you. I see it as a personal tool of self-discovery where you are uncensored in a messy process with the freedom to discover personal insights. It also provides a space for you to contemplate the theories you are introduced to, for example:

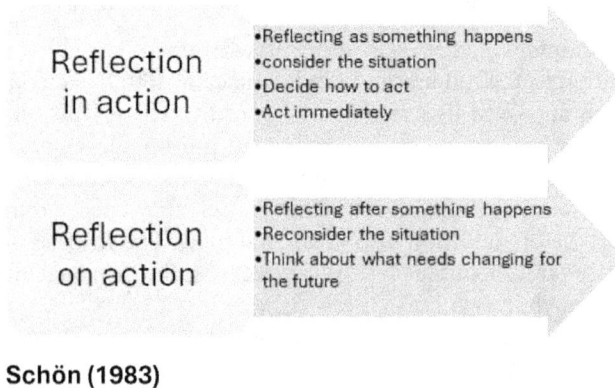

Reflection in action
• Reflecting as something happens
• consider the situation
• Decide how to act
• Act immediately

Reflection on action
• Reflecting after something happens
• Reconsider the situation
• Think about what needs changing for the future

Schön (1983)

Figure 1.2

I wrote about how much I hated Freud because suddenly everything had an unconscious meaning, and I was going round and round in circles about the meaning of everything I did. Then I found out that Freud had also said 'Sometimes a cigar is just a cigar' and I realised I had to accept my frustration. I was never going to find an answer to everything, and I didn't want to be a know it all anyway.

The higher-level courses require increased analysis of insights into your relational patterns including how these have developed through your upbringing and experiences as an adult. A typical learning outcome for a UG or PG Diploma or MA level personal development module might be: 'Examine/Critically examine your own relational patterns and the effect on others.'

Counselling requires you to be alert to all the information going on inside you (intrapersonal) and between you and the client (interpersonally). To be safe in such a profound and often intense relationship you will need to get more in touch with yourself. The word 'inter' from Latin means between, among, and during whereas personal from the Latin 'persona' means human being, a part in a drama or assumed character (Etymonline, 2023). This alludes to the complex nature of what arises in human relationships as we may present our 'safest persona' when we first meet someone and later reveal more of our true character once we feel more comfortable. There can be confusing interactions in groups as each person works out if they can trust the people in here and who their allies are. This self-awareness work often takes place in the personal development group setting.

The personal development group

On practitioner level courses which may be level 4 in a college or community setting, level 5 in a HE setting or level 7 (MA/PG Diploma route for those who already have a degree), it is usual for there to be a personal development group aspect. Within the group, trainees experience themselves with others and others with themselves. This mirrors similar processes to the counsellor-client relationship because you are monitoring how you feel when with the client and how the client may be feeling about you. These processes are part of your personal equipment that will help you to make therapeutic use of yourself when working with clients. Chapter 8 will explain this in depth, but it is stressed here that you are the person in the room with the client and so the more you know of how you seem to others, the more you can imagine your potential impact on the client. Equally the more you notice your reactions to others and make sense of these, the more you will be able to do this for your relationship with your client. The capacity to set aside prejudice and pre-ference is integral to fostering a safe non-judgmental space for clients to be real with you.

Can I be a client too?

To see yourself as a person in 'training' involves the willingness to accept what you don't know or at least to speculate that you may need to learn something. This involves a process of developing trust in yourself and appropriate trust in others. This development work can be accelerated through personal counselling. Most training providers require you to engage in personal therapy to support your openness to self-discovery as well as to cope with the emotional demands of introspection. Not all organisations expect this, but I would argue your role will be limited if you never experience counselling yourself, especially as in training you will be watching out for how the counsellor is working with you. I learned more about how object relations theory works in practice through being a client than through taught sessions in my training group! See Chapter 15 where I will look at the role of personal therapy in becoming a counsellor.

It's OK to be me

Counselling educators will be looking to raise awareness of your values and of your prejudices so that you may become self-aware and choose how to respond not from habit (speaking before you think) but from a considered and evaluated perspective. This can feel uncomfortable as the following example illustrates:

> Suddenly I'm questioning everything like who am I? and what have I been doing with my life? I feel like someone has dropped a huge stone in the middle of my pool of life and I miss the stillness of before, but I can't go back to that either now. I must keep going into new waters.

All levels of counselling training encourage you to talk about yourself and to share something about how you feel and what you think. This can feel exposing as I well remember from my early days in training. I was not used to being asked and felt on the spot and under pressure to come up with a smart intelligent answer. Other people seemed confident and much clearer than I did.

> To be honest, I often feel I have nothing interesting to say ...
> Being honest is always interesting said the horse.
> (The Boy, The Mole, The Fox, and the Horse)

Over time I realised I just had to be honest, to say if I didn't know or if I was struggling and even if I was feeling vulnerable. This was to be my development of genuineness, a key central facet of the counselling relationship and one that would ensure the other two conditions of empathy and unconditional positive regard could develop. After all, you have to get real with yourself to know what you feel and to put judgements aside, you need to face up to your prejudices.

How learning is facilitated

The use of micro skills and triads for practice

At the introductory level you will usually learn to practice the foundation counselling skills e.g., active listening, attending, paralanguage, contracting, paraphrasing, reflecting feelings, use of questions, use of silence and setting boundaries for the start and the end of a session. For a thorough list see McLeod & McLeod (2022) who offer an extensive list in a chapter 'A-Z of counselling skills' whereby responses to clients are grouped into those that help the client to tell their story, those that develop the relationship, those that enable reflection or choice and those that create a new experience.

Looking at this diagram, notice the difference between this one and Figure 1.1 on professional courses. Introductory levels focus on skills with a little theory and some self-awareness reflections. To provide a background to the teaching and practice of counselling skills we must give our thanks and gratitude to Gerard Egan (1975) who first presented the triad of counsellor, client, and observer. The practising of skills today and the micro skills approach has changed very little since they originally came into training most probably owing to the 'effective approach for teaching simple, clearly defined skills' (Connor, 1994, p. 7). The practising of foundational skills helps you to communicate what the American clinical psychologist Robert Carkhuff called the 'core conditions' (1969). These are Empathy, Unconditional Positive Regard and Congruence. All approaches to counselling place value on these aspects for building a safe relationship.

When students arrive at the first class for introductory levels, they are so excited to learn new skills that can develop their career. They are not perhaps prepared for the fact they will need to also be an observer and a client all of which develop different competencies required for the growth of the student counsellor.

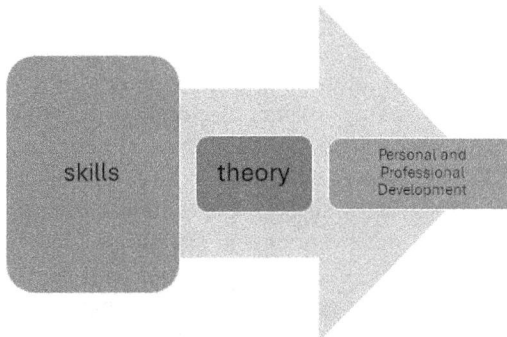

Figure 1.3

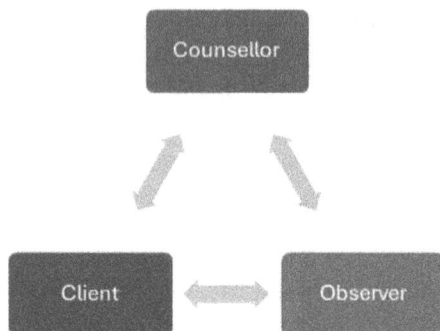

Figure 1.4 Triads

Triad work

- In the counsellor role – here you hope to develop empathy, a non-judgemental attitude, and genuineness as you listen to peers speak about their lives.
- The client role – here you are challenged to share aspects of yourself and how you feel and think to a helper. This brings the opportunity to develop empathy for yourself, non-judgemental attitude for yourself and to be genuine rather than guarded.
- The observer role – here you are challenged to be genuine in offering feedback in a respectful manner that is non-judgemental but constructive and to show empathy for the role of counsellor in helping the client. It is important that observers do not switch to analysing the client's problems. The client's problems are presented with a purpose – to help the counsellor to develop their skills. The feedback is normally for the counsellor only.

Typically, each skill is introduced by tutors via a description, example or demonstration prior to students practising. After practising you are guided to feedback on the experience. This implements the deliberate use of Kolb's experiential learning cycle (1984) where you have an experience in skills practice (concrete experience), you notice your thoughts and feelings (reflective observation), discuss those in the group and consider what all that means to you (abstract conceptualisation) then decide how you might practice next time leading to you trying something new (active experimentation).

It is important for counselling educators to build in time for feedback after skills practice so that the learning cycle can unfold naturally. Without attention to reflection on your observations and discussion of your thoughts about your experiences, there is a risk that you may not gain the insights needed to develop your counselling skills competency. We have many experiences every day but unless we take the time to consider the learning from those experiences, we may not learn anything at all.

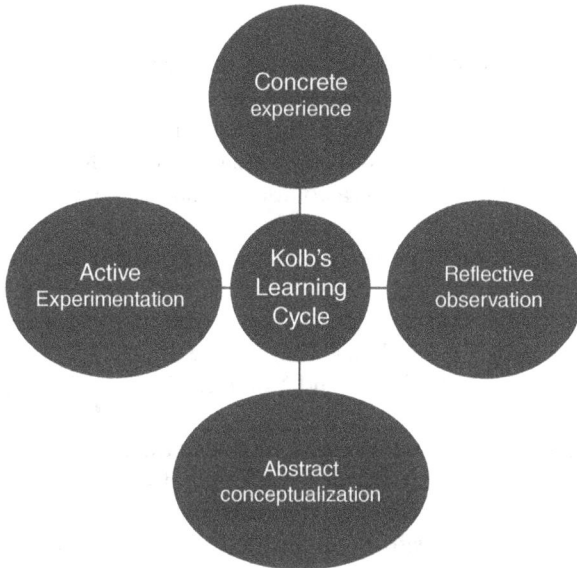

Figure 1.5 Kolb's learning cycle

As the levels increase you become more reflective both in action and on action as the typical learning outcomes below show:

- Introductory: (level 2) Demonstrate a basic ability to reflect on a range of counselling skills used to establish productive communication with a partner.
- Intermediate: (level 3 or PG Cert) Demonstrate an ability to reflexively offer a range of basic counselling skills in practice.
- Advanced: (level 4 or level 7, practitioner courses like Diploma/MA) Demonstrate an ability to use presence therapeutically, by articulating emotion, experience and personal meanings with empathy and authenticity.

Theory

At the introductory levels such as level 2 students are often surprised to learn there are theoretical foundations to the use of practising counselling skills. As the levels increase the more theory you will encounter. This is challenging for some people who feel they did not sign up for this theory/philosophy and psychology reading nor do they see how this is going to make them a 'good counsellor.' I usually reassure that once they are qualified it will not matter whether they got a 52% or a 75% and being good at academic writing does not mean you are any better as a practitioner. Those who struggle academically try to hold onto this perspective.

Why is theory important anyway?

Hansen (2006) speaks of the importance of theory to guide us in the practice of counselling. He highlights how theory is essential in helping counsellors organise clinical information that would otherwise be too complex to communicate and how theory provides conceptual guidance for interventions.

Imagine working in the NHS as a counsellor and you are asked to explain the reasons why your client needs 12 sessions instead of six or why you are asking the client to speak about their mother when they are bringing up issues with their wife. We need the correct professional language to explain to multidisciplinary teams such as social workers, consultants, occupational therapists or even our supervisors as to why we are doing what we are doing. The theory gives us a framework for working. Prochaska and Norcross (2018, p. 4) explain that

> without a guiding theory or system of psychotherapy, clinicians would be vulnerable creatures bombarded with literally hundreds of pieces of information in a single session.' They stress how theory helps by providing a 'consistent perspective on human behaviour' (and) 'the mechanisms of therapeutic change.
>
> (Prochaska and Norcross, 2018, p. 4)

Chapter 7 explains more about theoretical models and provides an overview of approaches for you to consider your reactions, beliefs and preferences.

Examples of teaching

The trainer/lecturer in their role of educator will create activities with the intention to engage the three domains of learning (Bloom et al., 1956).

- Affective domain – e.g., inviting you to consider how you feel i.e., your emotions, your attitudes
- Cognitive domain – e.g., what you think through remembering, defining and understanding
- Psychomotor (physical/kinaesthetic) domain – e.g., skills you can practice such as giving feedback and adapting your communication style

Example 1

Rather than being taught effective ways of giving feedback you may be asked to recall a difficult time when someone gave you some feedback that you found unpleasant.

- Where were you?
- What were the circumstances at the time?

- How did you feel?
- What did you do/how did you respond?

And to complete the process further...

- and what would you have preferred?
- what difference would that have made to you?
- what might the outcome of the interaction have been like?

The results of each person's responses combine to cocreate a useable framework for how to give feedback to each other in the group. This will then be supported by appropriate theory such as the feedback sandwich as first described by LeBaron and Jernick (2000) and perhaps how our mindset impacts on receiving feedback as identified by Carol Dweck (2007). Here a fixed mindset sees oneself as having a fixed potential that is limited to the hand you have been dealt with and a growth mindset allowing for failure sees feedback as a gift for further growth, learning and potential.

This is a typical learning activity/strategy in counselling training as the intention of the counselling tutor is to work with your head, your heart and your mind. This is important as you will be using the different parts of yourself to help your client.

Example 2

The following activity helps students to reflect on the challenges and support needed during their training. The task itself requires the sharing of personal experiences in a safe way and generates discussion of how theory may be applied to these considerations.

In your group discuss and decide:

- What do you think are the typical issues experienced by trainee counsellors?
- How may counsellors work with these issues in personal therapy according to their chosen theoretical approach?

During such an activity educators can offer feedback to support the discussion and check how students understand the different approaches to therapy. It presents the opportunity for deeper learning and a sense of commonality amongst group members.

Conclusion

This chapter has covered counselling and psychotherapy definitions and a brief overview of the training process to help you to decide the best route for you. It has explained the rationale behind the design of counselling levels and included examples of learning tasks and strategies to illustrate how they are typically facilitated. Overall, the purpose of key activities has been explored to help you be aware of the intentions of course design and assessment components.

References

ACA (n.d.) Licensure Requirements. Available from www.counseling.org/resources/licensure-requirements [date accessed 12 December, 2023].

BACP (2021) Introduction to counselling and psychotherapy. Available from www.bacp.co.uk/media/15699/bacp-introduction-counselling-and-psychotherapy-client-information-sheet-july-22.pdf [date accessed 24 April, 2025].

BACP (2022) SCoPEd framework A ground-breaking shared framework for our profession. Available from www.bacp.co.uk/about-us/advancing-the-profession/scoped/scoped-framework [date accessed 13 November, 2023].

Bloom, B. S., Engelhart, M. D., Furst, E. J., Hill, W. H., and Krathwohl, D. R. (1956) *Taxonomy of Educational Objectives: The Classification of Educational Goals. Handbook 1: Cognitive Domain.* New York: David McKay.

Carkhuff, R. R. (1969) *Helping and Human Relations,* Vols I and II. New York: Holt, Rinehart & Winston.

Connor, M. (1994) *Training the Counsellor: An Integrative Model.* London: Routledge.

Dweck, C. (2007) *Mindset: The New Psychology of Success.* Canada: Ballentine Press.

Egan, G. (1975) *The Skilled Helper: A Model for Systematic Helping and Interpersonal Relating.* Brooks/Cole Publishing Company.

Elkins, D. N. (2016) *The Human Elements of Psychotherapy - A Nonmedical Model of Emotional Healing.* Washington: American Psychological Association Press.

Etymonline (2023) Interpersonal. Available from https://etymonline.com/word/interpersonal.

Hansen, J. T. (2006) Is the best practices movement consistent within the values of the counselling profession? A critical analysis of best practices ideology. *Counselling and Values,* 50, 154–160.

Kolb, D. A. (1984) *Experiential Learning: Experience as the Source of Learning and Development.* Englewood Cliffs, NJ: Prentice-Hall.

LeBaron, S. W. and Jernick, J. (2000) Evaluation as a dynamic process. *Family Medicine,* 32(1), 13–14.

Macksey, C. (2019) *The Boy, the Mole and the Horse.* London: Penguin Books.

McLeod, J. and McLeod, J. (2022) *Counselling Skills: Theory Research and Practice.* London: Open University Press.

Norcross, J. C. (Ed.) (2002) *Psychotherapy Relationships that Work: Therapist Contributions and Responsiveness to Patients.* Oxford University Press.

OED (2025) Online English Dictionary. Available from www.oed.com/dictionary/counselling_n?tab=meaning_and_use#8059874 [date accessed 24 April, 2025].

Prochaska, J. O. and Norcross, J. C. (2018) *Systems of Psychotherapy: A Transtheoretical Analysis.* London: Oxford University Press.

Schön, D. (1983) *The Reflective Practitioner. How professionals think in action.* London: Temple Smith.

UKCP (2025) What is psychotherapy? Available from www.psychotherapy.org.uk/seeking-therapy/what-is-psychotherapy [date accessed 24 April, 2025].

Chapter 2

Motivations

Why counselling training and why now?

Jayne Godward

Introduction

> Why would someone want to listen, as a job and with no certainty of success, to people with a wide range of causes for unhappiness, depression and, at times, despair?
> (McBeath, 2019, p. 377)

What attracts people to this area? Why is counselling training so popular and a growing area?

This chapter aims to explore the reasons why this profession is chosen and to help you look at why you are choosing to train in this area. Often, it appears that the conscious motives are hiding other motives which students are not aware of at first.

We will explore some relevant research articles into therapist motivation and will look at the concept of the 'wounded healer' identified by Carl Jung (2014) and I will relate these ideas to my own experience and that of some current students on our training programmes.

It is important to be aware of our motivations as this can directly affect how we approach our work with clients and our effectiveness with them.

The chapter will include:

- an invitation for you to look at your motives for wanting to be a counsellor or psychotherapist
- A discussion about the importance of exploring our reasons for wanting to do this work
- an examination of recent research into this area
- an exploration of the wounded healer idea.

Why are we looking at motives?

It is really important to consider our motives for wanting to become therapists as this will affect everything we do when we are working with clients. It will affect how we approach our work with people, and it may

DOI: 10.4324/9781003405757-3

determine what model of therapy we train in. There is a real danger of unconsciously exploiting clients if we are not aware of our unknown and unmet needs.

Storr (1990, p.168) challenges us by asking: 'Are those attracted to the profession the best kind of people to become psychotherapists?' He goes on to look at how effective therapy has more to do with the therapist than the type of therapy offered. If the therapist is using their work to meet deep seated needs and to heal themselves, they may not always have the client's best interests at heart.

Occasionally at counselling training interviews I have met very vulnerable candidates who have more emotional needs than the clients they want to go on and help. So, if we are aware of our needs and motives and can examine and work on these, we are likely to protect ourselves and our clients from harm and be more effective practitioners.

Activity: What brings you here? Why counselling training and why now? Consider these questions.

- If you are already in the helping professions and volunteering with others what attracted you to that work?
- What has attracted you to counselling training now? Are there any links with your past history, life events and relationships?
- List your motivations for wanting to do this work. On the surface it may seem like a genuine altruistic wish to help others but be honest and delve deeper.

In Hawkins and Shohet (2012) the authors look at the shadow motives for those in the helping professions. These are summarised below. Did any of these apply to you when you delved deeper?

a   The wish for power – a need to be in control of our lives and the world around us. This may involve surrounding ourselves with people who seem to be worse off than ourselves and a need to direct the lives of the people who to us need help.
b   Meeting our own needs – here we need our clients to want our help – for our own self-esteem, i.e., the need to be needed.
c   The need to be liked and valued – do you want to be seen as a good person? But then how will you cope with clients who see you negatively or say you aren't helping them or who are generally ungrateful?
d   The wish to heal – this is often a basic wish for helpers and non-helpers.

We now go on to look at what the research into counsellor motivations says.

An examination of recent research into motives for wanting to be a counselling or psychotherapy practitioner

Although I had my own theories of why people chose to do this type of training, having interviewed many students and worked with undergraduate and post-graduate diploma groups since 2006, I did not presume that I knew but wanted to look at other people's views and research.

Although the research found is not comprehensive, it was relevant to this topic and fairly up to date. I give a flavour of this research below but recommend that you read these articles in full to understand them more. As you read about these findings, think about how these fit with you and your experiences and reasons for wanting to train.

From interviewing numerous students over the years my theory was that people don't just select counselling as a career choice out of the blue. They are drawn to it due to their personal histories or sense of vocation to help others which goes beyond altruistic and unselfish reasons. There is usually an underlying motive which is linked to a personal need in themselves. Often students are quite unaware of their real motives until they are actually on the training programme or even later on, but the personal development work on their course helps open up the Pandora's box as to why they are really there.

It may be useful to point out now that many of the famous founding therapists and theorists had troubled early lives and some continued to struggle with personal issues. For example, Jung and Melanie Klein suffered from losses, R. D. Laing had relationship difficulties and Eric Berne struggled in his personal life to mention a few. They didn't end up in their professions by accident.

Barnett's study in 2007 aimed to look at the 'unconscious motivation and gratifications of the would-be therapist' looking beneath the surface of a wish to help and understand others (p. 257). Nine experienced psychoanalytical and psychodynamic therapists looked at their professional and personal history. All of these had experiences of early loss prior to the age of 20 usually involving the loss of a father leading to the emotional absence of their mother due to depression and eight of these talked about their narcissistic needs. People tended to confide in them, and this confidante role became part of their identity. Sometimes this was a mother talking to their child and with others it might be peers.

The researchers found that feelings of isolation or introversion in childhood were common and that participants had a yearning to be close to someone or be important to someone. In all of them there was strong need for intimacy which had been lacking in some way in their childhoods. Seven of the participants had experiences of depression either their own or dealing with their mother's. It appears that the people in the study had unmet needs for closeness, intimacy and rather than them being dependent on others, others were depending on upon them, and their needs had to come first.

Interestingly Barnett suggests that the role of the therapist may offer a 'unique opportunity to experience an intimacy which has previously eluded them, especially as it is a "one-way only" type of intimacy, enabling them to remain at a safe distance, without personal involvement' (p. 260).

The therapists took on caring roles either to their peers or to their parents. Often, they developed sensitivity to other people's moods – becoming 'watchful children' (p. 268) wanting to avoid confrontation and upset. Most of them felt guilt because they were not good enough or loving enough or not meeting the expectations of the child their mother wanted.

The researcher talks about the theme of shame as participants struggled with parental disapproval, difficulties in changes in their environment, early trauma, family illness and secrets, parental limitations and family poverty.

The participants identified that there was a search for reparation – wanting to correct the situation which had occurred – the authors suggest that people become therapists to put 'the familial Humpty Dumpty back together again' (Barnett, 2007, p. 268)

This resonated with me and my history as my mother was ill with cancer from me being a child until 21 and I had a sense that I had to be a 'good girl,' not cause trouble and be there for her. Her needs would have to come first during some of my crucial developmental teenage years. I would go to appointments with her and would wait for her to come home. There was always a bit of a cloud hanging over me as to whether she was going to die soon or not. Luckily, I had a mature and solid father figure who I related well to, although he would be coping with the illness and working at the same time. The illness which was transformational to her personality, led to attachment difficulties and a sense of detachment from her. I also experienced feelings of guilt because I was not always sympathetic enough and felt I could have done more. Not surprising that I ventured into cancer support counselling later more for my own needs – wanting to face the demon of cancer and the trauma rather than from a rational perspective. Perhaps wanting to be there for others in a way I had not been able to be there for my mum. This proved to be a challenging venture (see Godward, 2007).

Barnett (2007) suggests that although the overt reason for wanting to do counselling training is a desire to help others, there may be a strong desire to be needed and an attitude of being able to work with any issue and any client. These are feelings of importance and omnipotence which can hide a student's vulnerability and compensate for feelings of humiliation and shame in childhood. The therapist might be striving for perfection and may develop an idealised image of themselves to protect themselves from their shortcomings and weaknesses.

Holliday, Peacock and Lewoski (2018) found evidence to back up the Barnett study in that they found that the students they studied on a child and adolescent psychotherapy course had experienced early relational adversity resulting in emotional distress which eventually led to them wanting to become therapists.

In this small-scale study, the participants had suffered relational adversity in the form of conflict between parents, bullying, loss of parental availability or had parents with mental health problems. There had been a conflict between what was expected of them and their own sense of self. This had led to distress including mental health difficulties. Some felt isolation and shame similar to that evidenced in Barnett's study (2007).

The key factor that led to these students choosing to train in child and adolescent counselling was that they had a positive restorative relationship with a particular individual and/or in group or community setting. The final theme identified by the study was an 'availability for and desire to create healthy relationships with others, particularly children and young people' (Holliday et al., 2018, p. 654) These authors identify this as altruism which arose from a sense of healing these participants experienced once they had overcome adversity. They say 'there is something redemptive in wanting something better for others and having a genuine desire to nurture others' (p. 655) This process is simplified below:

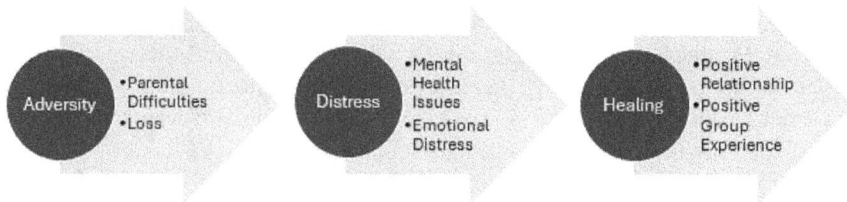

Figure 2.1 Process of development from adversity to healing

This backs up what I have found in many of my diploma students who having overcome difficulties have decided they want to give something back or empower other people to do the same. What seems important here is to meet the right person to help with this process of healing, whether this is an informal setting or in a more formal setting e.g., with a counsellor, teacher etc. The people in this study (Holliday et al., 2018) felt healed enough to begin training to be a counsellor. We will look at the idea of the wounded healer more below.

Three of my current students give the following accounts:

> In 2009 I used a psychedelic substance which caused a very intense bad trip which sparked a prolonged period of poor mental health. The following year I underwent CBT therapy to help me get control of this spiral that my mind was in but not before becoming deeply suicidal. The experience sparked a lot of deep reflection about what I had done with my life up to that point and I wanted to make more of myself. The care I received from my therapist inspired me to seek out a helping vocation of my own.

and:

> For me, receiving counselling, when I was experiencing tremendous stress in my life was transformative. Being able to express myself in a non-judgemental brave space, whilst being accompanied by an empathic and professional counsellor was hugely instrumental to my eventually being able to look at my own patterns and personal responsibility and from there, to slowly being able to make changes in my life, first within my inner world and then in the outer world.

and:

> I was first led to study this subject as a result of my personal experience of counselling. After an experience with CBT which left me feeling like I had firefighting tools but no understanding of what started the fire, I sought out talking therapy, so I could dig deeper and understand myself and my anxiety better. I found an integrative, but person-centred counsellor and started my journey. It was a profound and life changing experience for me. It made me more understanding, less judgmental and a lot more emotionally open. Discovering this level of emotional acceptance enriched my relationships and meant I was able to face the traumatic events which had shaped my life experience in a more considered way.
>
> This led me to the realisation that I had the potential to help others in the way I had been helped.

What stands out in the final two anecdotes is the importance of the non-judgemental or accepting space which allowed the students to heal and develop.

Most of the studies on therapists' motivations have been small scale with relatively few participants. The final study we will look at here was more wide scale. McBeath (2019) carried out an online survey of 540 psychotherapists to ascertain if the theories about motivation could be generalised. In his literature search, he had identified the following usually unconscious motives which other studies had highlighted which had arisen from the earlier experiences of the therapist:

- Need for admiration
- Need for intimacy
- Need to mask or deal with own fear
- Need for power
- Need to save or heal others
- Need to care for or nurture others

The therapists in this study came from a range of therapeutic models with 42% being integrative in approach and the sample appeared to be representative of the general counselling population.

The most popular motivation cited was the wish to enhance the client's growth (21%) closely followed by the motive of 'promoting self-growth' and the wish to learn about other people. McBeath sees this as a positive thing that whilst the participants wanted to help others, they recognised the need to work on themselves. Both go hand-in-hand in counsellor training usually in my experience.

Enhancing client growth	*21%*
Promoting self-growth	18 %
Learning about other people	16%
Professional independence	13%
Using therapeutic expertise	10%
Potential for self-cure	6%
Achieving intimacy	3%
Status	2%
Mystique of the therapist	2%
Hearing intimate details	1%
Power	1%
Other	8 %

Out of those surveyed 10% had had positive experiences of personal therapy. Other themes which came out of the study was the experience of mental health issues in the family, experiences of personal distress or trauma.

80% of those studied believed that unconscious motivations had played a part in their decisions to become therapists – 27% said to a large extent and 53% to some extent. Only 12% did not consider unconscious motives had a place in their choice of career (McBeath, 2019). Some of the findings are represented in the table below.

Here our interest is why therapists choose to enter this profession, however, it is also worth bearing in mind that motivations will change over time. One respondent said:

> I've been practising now for over 35 years. While not very admirable, my initial motives for training – self-cure and prestige – are probably still present to a degree and also inform my teaching and supervising. However other motives are also present now – pleasure in seeing people change, intellectual satisfaction, being touched by people's stories.
>
> (McBeath, 2019, p. 383)

The study did reveal that the therapists taking part identified with the concept of the wounded healer with many examples being given of some form of emotional disturbance which had eventually led to a decision to train in this area. This was also matched by the belief that these wounds could enhance their ability to be an effective therapist. We will look at this topic below.

The Wounded Healer

Carl Jung (1963) introduced the idea of the Wounded Healer by taking the Greek myth of Chiron and relating this to therapy. Chiron was wounded by an arrow dipped in poison and because he was immortal, he had to spend the rest of eternity carrying the pain around with him, looking for a cure. Due to the knowledge, sensitivity and capacity for empathy gained from his pain, he became a successful healer with transformative powers.

Jung suggested that we may be drawn to being therapists because of the pain we have faced in our lives and that our own hurt gives us the power to heal, but only by knowing our own pain can we be present with the pain of others.

It has been clear from the different research introduced in this chapter that therapists have often had difficult painful experiences prior to choosing this profession and may carry their wounds into training and beyond. The important thing is to be aware of our wounds and if possible, start to work on our own difficulties and pain before we begin working with real clients. However, often students are not aware of the depth of their pain until they enter a course and then the role of personal therapy, personal development and supervision become important otherwise their ability to help others may be impaired.

I strongly believe that we can only go so far with clients as we have gone ourselves. If we have not done the personal work, how can we expect the client to do this.

Two cases: Compare these wounded healers

Sophie

Sophie started a counselling course in her local community and then went on to do a practitioner course. She had suffered early childhood abuse and was keen to help others who had experienced this. She hadn't had any personal therapy but felt ready to do this work. She saw this as her purpose in life having come through her difficulties. On her first placement in a women's centre, Sophie was given a client who revealed severe sexual abuse between the ages of 5–10 years. After her first session with this client Sophie had a strong reaction. She was unable to sleep and started to have flashbacks to her own trauma. However, she carried on working with her client but was more cautious and avoided asking any probing questions which might delve into feelings. She kept herself professional but was a little cool with the client. After a few weeks her client stopped attending and said that she had felt that her counsellor was not interested in her and was too busy giving advice and coping strategies. Although Sophie's supervisor was supportive and encouraging, Sophie felt discouraged by what had happened and started to dread going in to see her clients. Eventually it all felt too much, and she decided to leave the course.

Ahmed

Ahmed started a counselling course in his local community and then went on to do a practitioner course.

He had come to the UK as a refugee from a war-torn country. He suffered from PTSD due to what he had witnessed and had eventually got help for this. He was now working for a housing association supporting asylum seekers and refugees. He had a settled life and a young family. He applied to do a placement within another organisation counselling refugees. At one of his first sessions, he had a young male client who had experienced a traumatic situation.

Ahmed was aware of the anxiety this triggered in him and took this to his supervisor and personal therapy. With the support of his supervisor, he approached his placement manager and said this was beyond his personal competence as a new trainee not trained in trauma work. He was then allocated clients who were more established in this country who were suffering from loneliness and isolation, feelings he had experienced and with which he could empathise without being emotionally overwhelmed.

Question: What are the differences between these two students? Both have had difficult and traumatic life experiences, but their situations are different in terms of being wounded healers.

The differences between our two students are the self-awareness and the ability to know their limits. Ahmed had already done some personal work on himself and had been able to help others in a work role. He made good use of his supervision and personal therapy to support him in doing this work. Whereas Sophie was keen to help others at any cost, particularly to herself, but had not worked sufficiently on her own emotional injuries to be able to support another person. She ended up protecting herself through her behaviour in the sessions, but this was not in her client's best interests, and she already was retraumatised by what she heard.

What our woundedness can give us is more humanity. It can be an equaliser in the counselling relationship. We are all in this together. Life does involve pain and suffering, and we are in the same boat with our client. We have anxieties, losses, relationship issues like our clients but we may just be a bit further down the road in understanding these and coping with these. That is what our counselling and therapy training gives us and the opportunity to work on ourselves.

Martin (2011) writes an interesting article about this. He talks about us being whole people. We are not pretending. We are bringing ourselves into the relationship with our client – we are imperfect beings doing the best we can as is the client.

He studied 17 therapists and asked them to talk about how their life crises affected their work with their clients. Some of his conclusions included that being wounded prevents us acting like an expert and enables more equality in the relationship.

Martin talks about 'embracing our woundedness in order to become more alive to one another' (Martin, 2011, p. 17) It is about being real and being human which will help us connect with clients and relate at depth. He talks about living with uncertainty and living better with 'fluid states.' This seems to be essential for counselling work where there is not a clear path either for the counsellor or the client during therapy.

In his conclusion to his study, he sees our mortality and woundedness as 'something to celebrate as a way to be more human, as a way of exploring compassion and life affirming joyous action and human intercourse' (Martin, 2011, p. 18).

Conclusion

This chapter has explored some of the possible motives for wanting to become a psychotherapist or counsellor. I have drawn on my own experience, that of students and the findings of research to hopefully stimulate reflection as a to why you want to enter this area of work. It is very important to consider why you want to do this work and to use this understanding to help you mitigate any motives which might have a negative effect on your counselling practice and even your ability to do the training. Personal therapy and supervision are recommended in this endeavour and self-awareness is essential.

We have looked at the interesting concept of the wounded healer and what this means, and I have proposed that rather than this being seen as negative term, if sufficient personal work has been achieved, a person can use their difficult experiences to enhance their work and their ability to relate to and help their clients. In fact, most of us are wounded healers and this is usually a positive in terms of enhancing our empathy and working with other members of the human race, i.e., our clients, in a more equal way. Accepting our woundedness and weaknesses can help us develop deeper relationships with our clients.

References

Adams, M. (2023) Recognising the Wounded Healer. *Therapy Today*, 34(7), 28–31.
Barnett, M. (2007) What brings you here? An exploration of the unconscious motivations of those who choose to train and work as psychotherapists and counsellors. *Psychodynamic Practice*, 13(3), 257–274.
Cleary, R. and Armour, C. (2022) Exploring the role of practitioner lived experience of mental health issues in counselling and psychotherapy. *Counselling Psychotherapy Research*. 22, 1100–1111.

Godward, J. (2007) Cancerland. *Therapy Today*, 18(3).

Hawkins, P. and Shohet, R. (2012) *Supervision in the Helping Professions*. Maidenhead: OU Press.

Holliday, C., Peacock, F., and Lewoski, C. (2018) Student motivations for undertaking a child and adolescent psychotherapy counselling course. *British Journal of Guidance and Counselling*, 46(6), 647–657.

Jung, C. G. (1963) *Memories, Dreams, Reflections*. New York: Pantheon Books.

Jung, C. G. (2014). *Collected works of CG Jung, volume 16: Practice of psychotherapy* (Vol. 52). Princeton University Press.

Martin, P. (2011) Celebrating the Wounded Healer. *Counselling Psychology Review*, 26 (1), 10–18.

McBeath, A. (2019) The motivations of psychotherapists: An in-depth survey. *Counselling Psychotherapy Research*, 19, 377–387.

Storr, A. (1990) *The Art of Psychotherapy*. Oxford: Butterworth-Heinemann.

Zerubavel, N. and Wright, M. O. D. (2012). The dilemma of the wounded healer. *Psychotherapy*, 49(4), 482–491.

Chapter 3

The selection process

To choose and be chosen

Jayne Godward

Introduction

The aim of this chapter is to explore the selection process which is likely to occur if you apply to train to be a counsellor or therapist. This is normally a Diploma course, either undergraduate or postgraduate. I will be examining what the interviewing tutors may be looking for but also, I will aim to encourage you to think about your own suitability and what you are bringing to the training and the profession at this time in your life.

Whilst drawing mainly on my own experience of selection, I have asked tutors from several different types of courses and organisations what they would be looking for in terms of personal qualities and attitudes and what would be the contraindications to acceptance and have included some of their comments in this chapter.

The selection process can be seen as a two-way process. The trainers are assessing your suitability, but you also need to assess if the training is the right one for you as there is a lot of variances between organisations as to what kind of learning experience they will offer.

In this chapter I will help you to understand:

- what is involved in the whole selection process
- why selection is important both for the training organisation and for you
- the personal qualities required to train and to become a counsellor
- what you will be asked about at the interview and what the interviewers are looking for.

Overview of the selection process

As a tutor who runs counselling diplomas, I think one of the most important but difficult tasks I have is the selection of appropriate students to our course. How can I determine whether a person I meet for 30–45 minutes is a suitable candidate for a demanding training programme? Even

DOI: 10.4324/9781003405757-4

with students I have taught on lower-level courses, it is still hard to decide whether this is the right time and choice, but it is even more challenging with a stranger. This is why interviews are normally undertaken with more than one interviewer to ensure balance and fairness. All course programmes will have entry requirements and specific guidelines which are laid down by the awarding body or institution but, even then, a judgement has to be made. I must draw on years of experience, intuition and the overall impression this person makes. Also, I need to be ethical and fair in my decision making.

Selection normally starts by reading the person's application form and looking at what they have done already both qualification wise but also work wise. If the person has already been a professional with a responsible job working with people, this would be seen as a positive. However, sometimes the applicant has not had this experience but can still be a successful candidate due to their life experience and because of their personality. At this stage I would say that most candidates will have had some experience of working with others in some kind of supportive role, either paid or as a volunteer and all applicants will have done their foundation training in counselling skills. This is a requirement for most training organisations and their awarding bodies. The UKCP, the United Kingdom Council for Psychotherapy specifically require that entrants to their accredited training programmes are graduates and have professional qualification or equivalent (UKCP, 2019).

We would also be looking at whether the person is at the right academic level to do a course. So, if a person has not got a degree already, they would not normally be able to do a post-graduate diploma/MA programme and similarly if a person had not done any previous counselling qualifications usually at Levels 2 and 3 they would not normally be going straight onto a diploma at either undergraduate or post-graduate level. We would also be looking at a candidate's ability to express themselves in a personal statement which is described below and to have a certain level of competence in their written language.

The personal statement

This is an important way of introducing yourself to your interviewers. You will be saying why you want to become a counsellor or therapist and why you are interested in this profession. You may also need to be clear on why the course you have chosen interests you. This will be linked into the approach being offered and the ethos of the training organisation. So, it is worth thinking about your motives carefully. Hopefully Chapter 2 helped you to look into this more and to examine how far you might be a 'wounded healer.' For my diploma course, we ask for the following:

> Why you would like to apply for this course and how you think it will benefit you personally and professionally. Please refer to the Person-Centred Approach in your answer.

Other courses are likely to want to know about your preferred approach to counselling and how you have been applying this in your work or life.

What we are looking for here is not that you want to become a counsellor, which is everyone's end goal, but how it will be of value to you personally and professionally. What will you gain from the course intrinsically – not just the qualification, i.e., how will it aid your personal and professional development? We also link it to our main approach partly to see if individuals understand this and what it might involve?

Usually in this statement, students talk about their previous course, normally a Level 3 Certificate and how this has helped them personally and professionally, which gives the interviewer a sense of how this person has been developing and using their studies. What comes across from appropriate applicants is the enthusiasm they have for this type of learning and for the subject area which is carrying them forward towards the Diploma. It is as if our applicants get the 'counselling bug' and want to carry on the personal learning and process. See the example below:

Extract 1: Personal statement

Another very important aspect of the certificate level was the written self-reflections. It taught me a great deal of what I am attaining from each topic and what my views and feeling are. I have also gained a good deal of self-awareness, how I unconsciously react to certain situations and my perceptions and judgements of the world around me.

I appreciate that the Diploma will be much more challenging in terms of self-perception, and I feel I am ready to do this. Before helping someone else, it is important to gain a better insight of yourself and own values and beliefs. I took a year's gap between the certificate level and the diploma so that I am fully prepared for the demands of the course. I feel now is the right time in every way for me to pursue my goal.

This person has gained a lot from their certificate (pre-professional level) and has taken time before coming on the Diploma to be ready for it. They aren't rushing into it. They are showing wisdom and have weighed up whether it is the right time to start the training.

Another candidate wrote:

Extract 2: Personal statement

Since beginning the counselling skills course in October, I have gained a real insight into myself and my interactions with others. Both personally and professionally I am becoming more understanding and empathic towards others – this is no longer restricted to people who I am familiar and/or friendly with. I have learned to listen actively, be empathic rather than sympathetic and allow people space to really dis-cuss how they are feeling and/or how a situation is impacting them rather than jumping in with condolences and advice. The most important thing I have taken from the course so far is the way I view myself, and consequently, others. Throughout my learning journey I have regularly reflected on my feelings or reac-tions to things (tasks or theories discussed in class, unexpected events in life etc) and I have much more self-awareness around my own feelings and shortcomings, which I am actively working on. Having this self-awareness has definitely benefitted me and allowed me to address issues which I thought I had overcome or gained closure on. [...] Understanding yourself and having acceptance of both your attri-butes and shortcomings is essential to being a successful person-centred counsellor as self-actualisation is a key concept in person-centred counselling. Therefore, I am striving to become a person-centred counsellor so I can support people in their own journey of self-actualisation through reflection and understandings of feelings and self so that they too can benefit from this process.

This person has been assessing their development since beginning foundation counselling skills training and is showing developments in both skills and personal interactions. They are showing that they have insight and are already moving towards practitioner training in their development and are ready to take the next step. They are also aware of what the person-centred approach involves.

Before or following your interview, the training organisation will need one or more references from people in some kind of position of authority with a good knowledge of who you are as a person. One of these is normally your Level 3 Certificate tutor.

This is important to me as a recruiter, as I am wanting to find out how the person coped with their previous counselling skills training and also what their reliability and commitment was like.

Activity: Your reference

Imagine you are your tutor or employer and need to provide a reference for yourself. How would you rate yourself on the following areas in the boxes?

Is the applicant?	*Comments:*
Honest	
Reliable e.g., attendance, meeting deadlines	
Punctual	
Responsible	
Patient	
A good communicator	
Emotionally able to cope with this level of training	
In good health both mentally and physically	
Interested in personal development	
Able to show empathy	
Able to ask for help if needed	
Able to accept constructive feedback/criticism	

Are there any areas where doubt might be cast on your suitability to train to be a counsellor? Or can you answer Yes or Good to all of these. N.B. the health question is a bit contentious but generally it makes sense for someone to be in good health at the beginning of the course. It might not be the right time if you are very unwell physically or not feeling emotionally robust at the moment.

References are important to tutors when they are selecting candidates that they don't know at all. They will be looking for reassurance that the person can make the commitment, work hard and that they have the sort of personality which makes them suitable to train and become a counsellor.

Most interviews are individual, with one or two tutors, however some organisations may do group interviews as well to see how you work in a group and how you communicate with others. Some training courses will require you to do a skills practice with a peer to ascertain whether you have the basic empathic skills to begin training. Finally, some courses may want you to do a written exercise on the day of the interview.

If the organisation requires you to provide lots of evidence of suitability, take this as a positive and feel proud if you are selected. However, if you aren't selected the first time you apply, depending on the feedback given, use this as a chance to work on yourself, gain more experience in using counselling skills or to look at whether this course was right for you or whether this is the right occupational area.

Why selection is so important

Imagine going on a professional training course where anyone or most people are accepted. What might be the consequences of this for the course, the tutors and the individual trainees?

Case study: Anwar

Anwar began his counsellor training at a large local training organisation. The course was eligible for student loans and there was pressure on the tutors to have large groups as course fees were kept low. Although Anwar had done all his preparatory skills training and was an experienced community support worker, he was surprised to find that some of his fellow students had been accepted without prior counselling skills training. In fact, it became quite frustrating because they did not know how to do a counselling practice skills session or how to use appropriate counselling skills. In the end he had to try to teach them what to do. One of his peers had only done an online remote training and was not used to working with others in groups and was really struggling. The group was very large, and it seemed overwhelming for the tutors.

As it turned out some of the students had been drawn to the course because they needed therapy themselves but wanted to help others in a similar situation to face their issues. They struggled with the personal development work and found it too emotional. Their difficulties and lack of resilience had not been picked up at interview and no reference was asked for from a previous tutor as they had come straight onto a Diploma.

Eventually Anwar became so disheartened by his lack of new learning and progress that he left the course. He had wasted a year in one respect and lost some of his course fee but had learned what to look out for if he applied for another training course.

This is based on true accounts of situations on some training courses. The moral behind this is to really research the different courses available to you. Notice what the selection is like. Is this thorough? Rigorous? Do you have all the information about the course before you apply? What are the sizes of the course groups. How many people teach on the actual courses? The cheapest courses may not be the best as the organisation may be taking a lot of students to keep the individual cost down but may also be budgeting on staff costs, so the ratio of student to tutor ratios could be high.

The selection process is for the student as well as the course team. You may not be suitable for certain types of practitioner training, but more appropriate for others. For example, if the course involves a lot of personal development work and you aren't interested in this, you may be better doing a different type of training or going down a different professional route.

Any questions about the nature of a course and how it is run can be asked about at open days or evenings or at the actual interview. Be prepared to ask questions to help you make an informed choice.

The interview: What qualities are we looking for?

Activity

Imagine you are a vulnerable client who has come to talk over a sensitive and personal issue with a counsellor.

- What sort of person would you want to speak to?
- What personal qualities would they need to have for you to trust them and open up about details you have not shared with anyone else?

Generally what interviewers are looking for are the qualities which means the person can undergo a personally demanding training programme at this time in their lives but also be the person who can go into placement and work with the vulnerable clients seen in counselling as in the activity. When we asked you to identify the sort of person you would want to speak to, you may have said:

caring, kind, honest, empathic, human, genuine, real, reliable, respectful and non-judgemental and someone who seems to know what they are doing who you can trust.

Some of these fit with the core conditions in Person-Centred counselling of respect, genuineness and empathy, (Mearns and Thorne, 2013) whilst others align to the personal moral qualities identified by the British Association for Counselling and Psychotherapy's Ethical Framework (BACP, 2018).

These are laid out as candour, openness about harm or risk, care, courage, diligence, empathy, fairness, humility, identity, integrity, resilience, respect, sincerity and wisdom (BACP, 2018, pp. 10–11).

Similarly, the UKCP say that organisations have 'systems to demonstrate that they have personal qualities that make them suitable for the psychotherapeutic counselling profession' (UKCP, 2019).

So, these essential personal qualities are fundamental in that the applicant will need to build relationships with colleagues in their course group and with clients in their counselling practice and with other workers when on placement. As an interviewer I would be expecting to see some evidence of these either in the written application, personal statement and references as well as in the interview.

At this point I want to say that the interviewers for practitioner courses could be seen as the gatekeepers to the profession and to an extent we have an ethical responsibility to maintain standards and to protect clients as well as vulnerable applicants from harm. Embarking on a training course where you are usually expected to work on yourself, interact with other vulnerable people and go out and listen to sometimes harrowing experiences is not the best thing for someone who is not emotionally robust or does not possess some of the personal qualities identified above.

Activity: Reviewing your personal qualities

How would you score yourself from 1–5 on these (where 1 = needs a lot of improvement and 5 = very good)?

For each of these think of an example of when you have demonstrated this quality in your relationships with people either voluntary or paid and/or with your family and friends.

- Care
- Courage
- Diligence
- Empathy
- Fairness
- Integrity
- Resilience
- Respect
- Sincerity

I have chosen nine personal moral qualities to help you think about how you relate to others and how you demonstrate the ability to deal with personal or professional challenges.

The interview: What will you be asked about?

Generally, there are some key areas which you will be asked about. See the diagram below:

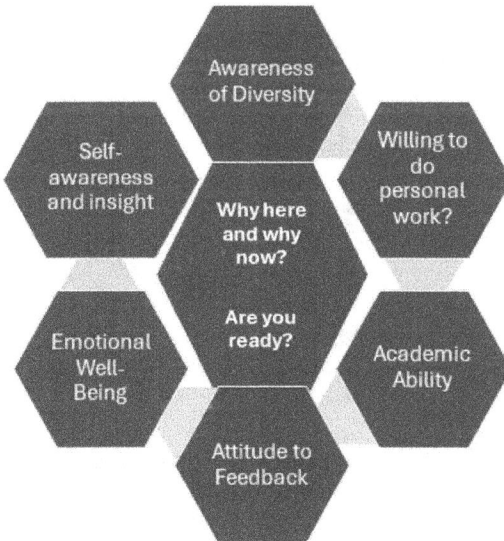

Figure 3.1 Interview topics

Why are you here and why now? Are you ready?

Usually, I am really interested to know why a person wants to become a counsellor or do the training. What has brought them at this point in their life? The majority of applicants have had personal issues or difficulties in their lives, which has led to them being drawn to helping roles especially working with clients with similar issues or their experience has made them interested in understanding people more due to a hidden motive to understand themselves more. We have looked at this in more detail in Chapter 2 when we look at the 'wounded healer' idea.

Very few trainees have had an emotionally pain or carefree life so far. Generally, this manifests itself in wanting to help others. Some have been told that they are good at listening to others or that they are seen as approachable by others. Many of our applicants are already in professional health or social care roles, such as nursing, social work, community support or work as volunteers for charities. It is usually no coincidence that they are already in these helping roles.

Here I want to stress that having had issues and having had counselling yourself is generally seen positively rather than negatively, provided that you are functioning well emotionally and are feeling robust at the present time. So, the tutors will be checking this out at the interview. They are looking out for any signs that your mental or emotional health might be a barrier to you interacting in a group or more importantly working with vulnerable clients. Obviously, this can be hard to assess but expect to be asked about significant life events or relationships and how these have impacted on you personally and whether you have had counselling before and the circumstances, so that you can give any relevant information.

Normally people are forthcoming with this and usually they are in a good place. I think it is important to be honest with your interviewer and work with them to assess if this is the right time or right course for you.

Activity: What would you do?

Imagine that you are the interviewer. Do you think these applicants are emotionally robust? Is it the right time for them to begin this training?

Marie is a shop manager who is currently studying her Level 3 certificate. She has suffered from depression for many years but after having counselling in her 40s she realises that the root of her health issues was her poor relationship with her mother, who was an alcoholic and was often neglectful. Marie often felt unsafe and was often criticised, leading to her having low self-esteem. Through counselling she pieced together aspects of her past and started to realise why she felt bad about herself. Gradually she has built up her self-esteem and has been working as a volunteer for a local mental health charity supporting others with depression.

Jamil is a 30-year-old teaching assistant and father of two. He works hard in his role and really likes to help the children to learn. He is very keen to do your diploma course as he wants to become a professional counsellor working with children and is currently taking a Level 3 certificate. In the interview he talks about a recent distressing incident where he was assaulted in the town centre. He looks visibly upset as he tells you about it. He hasn't had counselling but has talked a lot to his sisters who have been supportive. He would be willing to have counselling before the course starts if that was required.

You will see from these that it is very difficult to judge emotional stability and sometimes tutors take a risk to give someone a chance and sometimes this may also be the wrong decision. The problem is that if someone is already wobbly emotionally the course with its personal development aspects may just nudge them over. As tutors we are trying to prevent harm to the candidate and their clients following the ethical principle known as non-maleficence (BACP, 2018).

What commitment can you make?

When I interview people for a counselling diploma course, I am keen to find out if they can make a sufficient commitment to it, as a lot of time is required. In the past we would say to allow at least two days a week to do the programme even if the training is only on one afternoon and evening or a full day per week. This is to allow for attending placement one half day or evening a week, attending supervision regularly, and having the personal therapy if this is required by the Course. You also need time to study and for personal processing time. The diagram below sums this up:

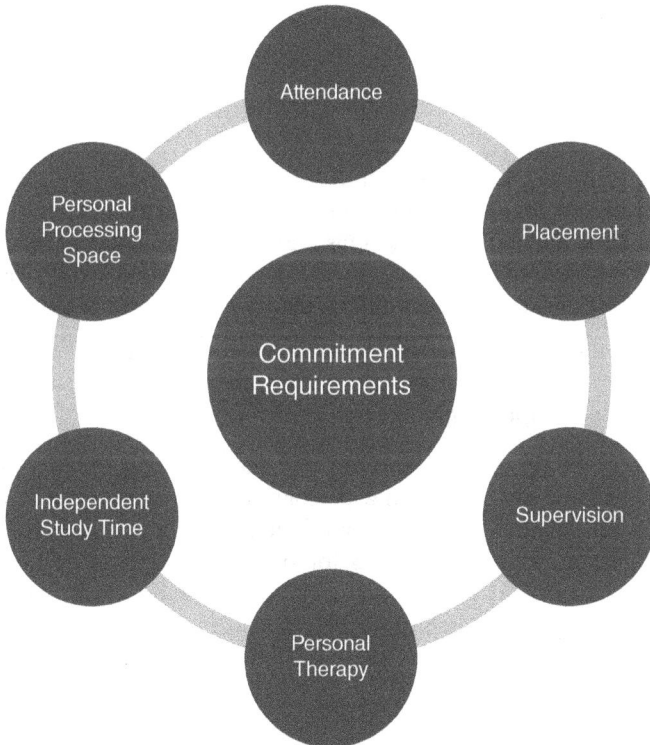

Figure 3.2 Commitment requirements

Self-awareness and insight

We are looking for candidates who already have some personal awareness and who have usually done some personal development work as part of their counselling skills training or in their personal therapy. This is why the earlier levels of the foundation training at Levels 2 and 3 or post-graduate certificate are important as they can prepare you for what is to come. If an applicant really lacks self-awareness or evidence of personal development work, they may not be ready to do the training. If they are not able to answer questions about themselves, their relationships or their previous experiences with some insight, this might not be a good time or a psychotherapy/ counselling training might not be the right training for them. Usually, people with self-awareness can answer questions on their personal qualities and areas for development.

When asked what a contraindication for acceptance would be, tutors said the following:

> Somebody who lacked personal maturity or who did not have any insight. They would not be able to look at them self in any depth and would possibly be quite defensive about opening up or talking about themselves, except at quite a superficial level.
>
> (Post-Graduate Diploma tutor)

and:

> I want to invite their vulnerabilities and shadow selves into the interview process, that will give me an insight into the applicant as a person, in addition to their previous qualifications and work experience. Despite meeting the course requirements, if I am met with resistance and avoidance from the applicant, I may chose to not offer a place on the course or an alternative.
>
> (Tutor in Children and Young People therapy course)

Willing to do personal work?

As we explore in this book there are personal challenges doing counsellor training as usually you will be in a personal development group and will be expected to talk about yourself and really look at who you are and why you behave in certain ways. There is a lot of self-exploration expected. Most courses also expect you to have some personal therapy. You may be asked about your willingness to engage in these activities.

Academic ability

Psychotherapy and counselling courses vary in the amount of academic work which is expected of their students. If you are choosing an undergraduate diploma, there will still be a lot of written work to produce but the academic level will not be as in-depth as a post-graduate course, in terms of the amount of reading and research required. Both types of courses will have similar demands in terms of personal and professional development.

Awareness of diversity

It is very important that you are willing to work with people from a range of backgrounds and perhaps can demonstrate your ability to do so. You may be asked about this at interview. Think about your experiences of working with different types of people and any challenges you might have had. You may be asked about how you have become more aware of your identity and beliefs during your counselling training so far, so be prepared to answer questions on this. We look more at this more in Chapter 5.

How are you with feedback?

On a counselling or psychotherapy course, you will receive feedback as to how you come across to others and how you work with your peer clients in skills practices. This will help you grow and develop and is an essential part of the training. For this reason, you may be asked how you respond to feedback and challenge and possibly how you have used this for your development. What interviewers are looking for here is someone who is willing to listen to feedback, not be defensive and really use this to improve. It is ok to be honest and say you struggle with it but are really willing to work on this. It is important to recognise that being a counsellor is not about being perfect or doing a perfect job as both are impossible. Clients don't want a perfect counsellor but a real person with whom they can share their difficulties without feeling judged.

How do you relate to others?

Finally, the whole interview will be assessing how you communicate and relate with others. From the moment you meet your interviewers or switch on your camera to enter the interview space, you are making a connection, and the process starts. As the ability to relate and make connections is central to counselling practice and to working in groups on your chosen course, it is important to put yourself across in a friendly, approachable and personable way and be willing to talk about yourself and answer the questions as fully as possible. We realise that this is difficult when you are nervous, but all interviewers allow for this and are fair about this. Just try to be as relaxed as possible, try to smile, be friendly, genuine and non-defensive.

Tutor views on this were:

> I would look out for genuineness in answering any questions, including a willingness to share both strengths and vulnerabilities.
>
> (Children and Young People therapy tutor)

and

> Contraindications have been defensiveness that is beyond jangly nervousness, aggression, severe lack of general awareness, lack of prior qualifications, shallow self-awareness.
>
> (Undergraduate Diploma interviewer)

My reactions to interviewees have varied from: 'What a lovely person, they were so warm and open' to 'that was hard work, they didn't give a lot away' to 'we couldn't get them to shut up, they took over and needed to control the interview' or 'I felt like I had to look after them, they seemed to be more like a client than a would-be counsellor.'

Conclusion

I hope this chapter has helped you understand what is involved in the selection process for counsellor or psychotherapy training and, in particular, what is being looked for at the interview stage. I have focussed on certain personal qualities and attributes which will be required but I have made it clear that it is not about being all sorted out and not having any issues or about being perfect, it is about being good enough and emotionally robust enough to embark on the training at this time. Everyone is unique and we all bring something different to this profession warts and all!

References

BACP (2018) *Ethical Framework for the Counselling Professions*. Lutterworth: BACP.

Godward, J., Dale, H., and Smith, C. (2020) *Personal Development Groups for Trainee Counsellors: An Essential Companion*. London: Routledge.

Mearns, D. and Thorne, B. (2013) *Person-Centred Counselling in Action*. London: Sage.

UKCP (2019) *The Minimum Core Criteria for Psychotherapeutic Counselling with Adults*. London: UKCP.

Chapter 4

The personal challenges of counsellor training

Jayne Godward

> The world is full of helpers whose activity is a desperate strategy to avoid confronting themselves.
>
> (Mearns and Thorne, 2011, p. 44)

Counselling or psychotherapy training is unlike anything else you will undertake and as we will keep emphasising in this book, requires personal demands on the trainee. This makes it both challenging but also very rewarding. For me the greatest gift I gained from my training wasn't the ability to go and practice with clients but the level of self-knowledge I gained from the personal development aspects of the Course.

Many applicants for counselling training have worked in emotional supportive roles either as a volunteer or a professional. Within these roles there tends to be more of an emphasis on 'doing to' and of keeping a distance rather than the approach in counselling which is usually about 'being with' and emphasises the importance of self- awareness, being authentic and using yourself in the therapeutic relationship. To do this, students are required to really look at themselves and to do personal development work, which brings challenges not encountered in other professional training.

In this chapter I felt it would be useful to share my experiences of this process then go on to talk about those of the students which I have taught.

This chapter will include sections on:

- why self-awareness is important in counselling work
- my experience as a trainee doing the self-awareness work
- the impact of woundedness on the trainee
- the personal challenges students face during training from a trainer and a student's perspective.

The importance of self-awareness in counselling work

Often when students apply to do counselling courses, they think this will be just an extension of their current roles where they are already helping and

DOI: 10.4324/9781003405757-5

supporting other people, with the counselling skills training giving them another string to their bow. What they don't realise is that a lot of the personal development work on the study programmes, especially at the higher levels will involve them really looking at themselves and endeavouring to be more self-aware. They may think gaining insight into the self is just something to help their potential clients with and don't realise that they need to go through that process themselves. Even when we warn students about this challenging aspect of the training at interview, they are still unprepared for what is to come.

Ponder point

Why do you think we need to look at and understand ourselves before we can work with others as counsellors?

To answer this question, I will use another question. What would it be like to go to see a counsellor who has limited self-awareness when you have come to see them to discuss a difficult personal issue in a relationship?

When you enter the room, the person looks ill at ease and is fidgeting. Or you enter the room, and they are immediately sounding gruff and bossy. (They need to feel in control.) They even look a bit smirky (due to their nerves) when you start explaining your problem.

This person is lacking in self-awareness and can't manage their discomfort. This may mean you would not want to open up to them as a client as they do not seem non-judgemental or trustworthy. There is also an inauthenticity about them.

To offer counselling you need to feel secure enough in yourself to be able to enter a relationship with another person. Doing the personal development work on your course will help you look at your emotional difficulties, your personality, values and beliefs, behaviour and hopefully will help you develop more trust in yourself. Low self-esteem and self-worth is not uncommon in society and many of us suffer from this at some point in our lives but the training can help us to accept ourselves, flaws and all and can help us look at the negative experiences we have had in the past and give us chance to work through these in a supportive environment in the class sessions or in our personal therapy, often a requirement of psychotherapy and counselling training.

Mearns and Thorne (2011) talk about the importance of self-acceptance and self-love and that how we relate to ourselves will determine how we relate to our clients in the counselling relationship. Part of therapy training involves becoming more in touch with our real selves, stopping pretending or putting on an act and starting to be more genuine. This is important in the counselling relationship as if your client feels like you are honest and genuinely interested in them and their progress and not being false, they are more likely to be honest and open with you.

All this is easier said than done as becoming more in touch with your real self means looking at areas we would rather not acknowledge or accept. What is sometimes referred to as our shadow side. These may be things we have rejected, denied or never realised about ourselves (see Jung, 1991).

In Chapter 11 you will see that the counselling relationship is a unique relationship where the therapist draws on their personal resources to be fully present and available to their clients.

We also need self-awareness, so that we do not impose our views and agendas on clients, as in most counselling approaches the counsellor is not saying what is good for the client or advising but aiming to empower and give the person autonomy. Whereas in other roles we would be advising, treating, teaching and doing unto the person we are working with, thus the relationship becomes more top-down where we are in an expert position, and they are in an inferior position. A counsellor lacking self-awareness may subtly impose their agenda on the client or manipulate the outcomes of sessions. This would prevent them providing the non-judgemental space which is required for the client to examine their issues.

Case study: Jason

Jason thinks he is working in a person-centred way. He allows his client, Phil space to talk and shows empathy for his emotions and difficult situation. However, when Phil starts revealing that he is secretly going out with his friend's wife, he becomes uncomfortable and starts to ask direct questions about the friend and whether he suspects. In another session, he diverts the topic away from this subject when his client starts talking about it. In supervision he realises that there is a real block to empathy and unconditional positive regard emerging as Jason recently had a breakup from his girlfriend where she went out with his best friend and is now living with him.

He starts to wonder if he can work with the client if the experience being presented is so triggering for him and discusses this further in supervision. In the end he does continue to work with Phil but learns to put to one side his experience and really focus on the client's story and feelings.

It turns out that Phil's wife has been mean and coercive for years and his friend's wife has been supporting him emotionally and cares about him but still loves her husband so is not intending leaving him. Phil was having stronger feelings for her but needs the counselling space to explore what is really going on. With the support of his supervisor and the personal therapy he is required to have on his course, Jason is able to look at feelings from his past experience which he had not come to terms with which could block him from being present with clients, including feelings of anger, rejection and loneliness.

The other advantage of becoming more self-aware is that we are less likely to become burnt out or rush into work with clients who are too personally challenging as we know our limits and can monitor our fitness to practice. Self-awareness helps give us some protection against the demands of our work.

Activity: What do you know about yourself so far?

Below are some areas you will find useful to consider before or as you begin counselling training. Your exploration of these is likely to continue throughout your training and beyond and the answers may change over time.

- How am I with emotions? Which emotions are acceptable to me in myself and which ones are acceptable to me in others? Are they the same or different?
- How ready do I feel at this time to look at aspects of my past which are painful which may cause me emotional distress?
- What is my sense of worth? How do I feel about myself?
- What are my fears and anxieties? What are my biggest worries at the moment?
- What are my values and beliefs? How do they inform my life at the moment?
- Who am I in this world? What does my identity look like? How would I describe myself?

My experience as a trainee

Before training to be a counsellor I had already done nurse training, a degree and teacher training so I was used to being on academic courses and used to the rigour of professional training where there were practical assessments and observations as well as written assignments. I had for a long time been interested in psychology and aspects of my social science degree covered this, so I was not new to looking at people in this way.

So, what was different about doing counselling training for me personally?

The big difference was the personal exploration and the increased awareness of relationship and emotional issues which were uncovered – my shadow aspects.

Funnily enough at this time I did think I was quite mentally sorted and that I did not have many personal issues which would get in the way of the actual counselling or training. It was only later I realised that there was a lot lurking in my emotional store cupboard.

The first challenge for me was joining a new group. Old fears from the past came up – would I be accepted? Would people like me? How would I fit in?

Due to a difficult time in upper school where I felt different and had few friends, the ugly beast of doubt raised its head – the one that hinted that I was not likeable. I had already done some work on being more accepting of myself, but I was suddenly taken back to this by joining a new professional course which was populated by people who were usually older than me and people who were already professionals in their own right. The old inferiority complex reared its head. So, for a time I would be managing the anxiety linked to this but gradually forming relationships and feeling like I belonged which I think is important for students in counselling training groups. Feeling accepted is such a crucial thing if we are to move forward in this sort of training.

The first major personal hurdle came with the residential weekend. On many courses at that time there tended to be a residential aspect where you went away for a weekend with your peer group and did some intense personal group work. This weekend was very difficult for me, as I felt intense anxiety being away from my partner and the work we did was about attachment and loss among other things. On this weekend I tapped into some intense emotions of separation anxiety, loneliness and loss and spent most of the weekend in tears. It was a mixture of the content and the physical separation experience which was painful. Most students uncover and have realisations but usually in a gradual way on courses, but the weekend experience was a deluge rather than a 'drip drip' experience. I hadn't been aware of these aspects of my personality and the issues I had with attachment and loss due to my own personal history of losing my mother whilst being a young adult. I had buried these things. I was able to go on and take these to my personal therapy, which was a requirement of the course and continued to look at these.

The personal therapy was very useful and very painful at times. I spent a lot of time crying and working things out but the insight I gained from this has really helped me to move forward in life and in my work as a counsellor. In a way it was like a cleansing process but very painful.

I can't emphasise enough in this chapter that doing therapy training is hard work emotionally and requires a resilience to keep going even when it feels tough. This is why students need to feel robust and stable enough at the beginning to cope with this.

My account shows a massive difference between doing other types of courses and training in psychotherapy and counselling. The real challenge is to learn about yourself, face up to aspects of your personality which have been packed away or repressed and start to work on these difficult things. This is a lot to ask but is necessary if you are going to be an effective practitioner within a counselling relationship. In the other work I had trained in, you could hide behind a professional façade and put on a bit of an act, but in counselling there is a requirement, especially in person-centred counselling, of being yourself.

The assignments we did on the course also demanded some personal input unlike those written on other courses. You were expected to write from the first person, 'I' point of view rather than the third person and you needed to link your experience to the theory you were learning. There is no distancing yourself from the material you are studying just as there is less professional distancing from the people you are working with.

For example, in nursing, I would care for dying people or those with serious diseases, but I wore a uniform, and I would sit and talk to people at times, but I could keep the professional distance and would not be working with them so much on the emotional level rather than the caring/practical level. I would be doing things for people and could hide behind reassurances rather than deep empathy for that person, which is more personally demanding.

In counselling, you are entering into the worlds of people and your main role is to be there with the person in their distress and to really understand this with them. An element of genuineness and realness is required if they are to trust you with their inner thoughts and feelings. This also brings the challenge of their material touching yours and the need for you to be really aware so that your issues don't interfere with your work and responses.

My experience as a tutor: What are the personal challenges students face?

In this section I will draw on my experience as counsellor trainer in HE and FE/Private Training Organisation for the last 18 years and will look at *some* of the personal challenges which have arisen for the students I have taught. I will categorise these into two areas: woundedness and relational issues and how these manifest in training, although they do overlap.

Woundedness and its impact on the trainee

In Chapter 2, I discussed and looked at motivations for wanting to become a therapist. One of the clearest themes was that people come into this profession because of a personal need they have to help others due to their own experiences of difficulty. The wounded healer idea was examined. Most of us enter the profession as wounded healers and bring this woundedness on to the counsellor training. If I look around one of my current diploma groups, no one has had a carefree easy-going life up until now. Everyone has had challenges to face which led to them opting for this career route. The important thing is how far have people addressed their woundedness prior to starting training? Are they ready to do the personal development work on the course?

If you haven't had personal therapy or done personal work on yourself, you need to be prepared for some difficulties as you start the personal development work on the course.

Below we look at some of the needs that McBeath (2019) identifies from his literature research into the motives of psychotherapists and how these can manifest on a counsellor training course.

Need for admiration

Students may feel a need to show that they know what they are doing and that they are making progress. They may talk a lot in the groups or want to get praise from their tutor or peers. This may be because they did not get a lot of this from their parents or significant others when they were growing up. They may want positive feedback from their clients and reassurance that they are doing a good job. This may not be possible so it may be difficult if they feel like they haven't had a good outcome with a client or where things don't go how they wanted it to go.

Need for intimacy

In Chapter 2, it was suggested that counsellors who lacked intimacy in their early lives, may seek a type of intimacy with clients which really is one way and is 'safe' in that they don't need to reveal much of themselves but form a close therapeutic relationship with a client. If students have become used to being the listener or carer but not used to sharing aspects of themselves, this may be a real challenge on a counselling course where you are expected to talk about yourself and your experiences.

Need to mask or deal with own fear

Admitting fears or anxieties may be seen as a weakness to some students and in the past they may have had to 'be strong' to cope with challenging personal situations. As a result, showing vulnerability or expressing what could be seen as 'negative feelings' may feel difficult either in the course group or in personal therapy. Sometimes this is linked with conditions of worth (see Mearns and Thorne, 2011, pp. 11–12) when they were younger where they had to be brave or strong to gain approval from others and where talking about fears was not acceptable. For example, in some families crying or being angry would be frowned upon, so students will struggle to do these in a course group or when being a 'client' in skills practice. Some students may feel shame about this or may find it intolerable to be upset in this way. Instead, they may put on a brave face or be unauthentic when genuineness and being real is what the training is encouraging.

Need for power

If in your early life you have lived in unpredictable or unstable conditions, there may be a real need to be in control or to have power over yourself or others. Hawkins and Shohet (2012) suggest that we become carers to gain some control and may surround ourselves with people who are worse off than ourselves so that we can direct their lives.

Need to save or heal others

I have come across this saviour complex in some students who want to save or help others in a way that they would have liked to be saved themselves when they were young. As a wounded healer, they are using this to restore themselves. This might be shown in students when they try to help their peers in skills practice rather than just listening or really empathising. There is a real urge to make it better or to rescue the other person. An example is given here as it is quite a common trait in new trainees and may be a difficult to overcome.

Case study: Sally, the saviour

Sally had a difficult childhood, where she suffered emotional abuse from her parents and developed a low sense of worth. Later she developed her confidence through helping others in her work as a mental health support worker and later as a mental health nurse. She identified with people who were struggling psychologically and wanted to help them to feel better. This led to her choosing to train to be a counsellor. What tended to happen in her skills practices was that rather than just attending to the client and allowing them to reflect and express feelings, she tended to jump in with solutions and really struggled when her peers cried or became angry about their situations. Her natural tendency was to go into rescue mode. That is rescuing them from intense feelings.

The same pattern occurred in her personal development groups where she would want to make it better for a peer who became upset by offering tissues, hugs or answers to their dilemmas. It was very difficult for her to sit with their distress as it triggered memories of her own distress from her past. Her tutors were concerned that she would show this same behaviour when working with real clients and suggested she attended personal therapy to help her look at what had happened in her past and the emotions she struggled with.

Need to care for or nurture others

This is similar to the point above; however this need is linked to being useful and having value. Helping others in our counselling work may give us a purpose and help us to feel worthwhile. Hawkins and Shohet, (2012) talk about the need to be needed and to be liked and valued as shadow motives which we might not be aware of when entering counsellor or therapy training. This can cause issues for students generally as they are so used to being the carer or the person people come to for help that it is difficult to set boundaries. This can impact on them doing the course and finding time for themselves or their studies. It can also mean that if they have difficulties with clients or sessions don't go well, they will take responsibility for this rather than seeing it as a relationship where the client has to take responsibility for engaging and doing the work of therapy.

Relational issues

Personal values and beliefs

A key part of counselling training is to learn how to relate to a range of people from different backgrounds with different values and beliefs. In the group you will hopefully meet people who are very different from you but also those who are similar and interestingly those who remind you of people from your past or present relationships.

To unpick this further there may be personal difficulties related to your strongly held beliefs and values. These beliefs may be religious, political, linked to your culture and how you see the world. Until we enter a group with different people, we are not always aware of how strong our views might be. Interacting with diversity helps us to understand who we are but is also very challenging personally.

My colleague said that one of the hardest things to come to terms with in her training was that two polar opposite views can exist in the same space, for example:

Case study: Poles apart

Gina has a strong catholic faith and is influenced by her Christian values. She finds the blasphemous language in the group difficult at times. Jenny is an atheist and expresses strong views on this. She thinks "the whole religion thing is a con" and was a way of keeping people oppressed in the past and still in the present in some societies.

- How can these two opposing standpoints exist in one place?
- How will these two students exist together in their group?

It is as if they are both standing on the opposite sides of a massive river.

The point is that both people have their convictions and no one in the group including the tutors have a right to say what is correct or not. Nobody is wrong, both views are valid. As a group member or as a tutor we don't need to agree with either person, what we need to do as we would in a counselling session, is be interested in where the person is coming from and why these values and beliefs are important to them. We need to empathise with them and respect their views but don't need to agree with them.

I see the empathy and respect like a bridge. We can walk across and talk to them but we don't have to join their camp. There is no need for conformity or consensus in the group about what we think and believe.

Our values and beliefs make us who we are and make up our individual identities, I, personally, don't want everyone to be the same.

If I visit a different culture on my travels, I want to understand what they believe and think and why they live in that way, but I don't want to adopt that way of life, but I can take away more knowledge and understanding.

The difficulty students have is when they want people in their group to conform to how they want them to be. A student may have a fixed idea about how a counsellor should behave or what is acceptable or not. Part of the training is to start to accept people who don't behave like you or people who have traits you find difficult. This is helpful for client work where we can't impose our values on others.

Case study: Sasha and Jay

Sasha came to this country from America. She has a strong religious background and feels deeply about how people should behave towards others. She has been finding another member of her group obnoxious, as the woman, Jay talks a lot, is very loud and has strong views. Sasha does not think this is a professional way to behave and it is alien to the culture she has come from.

Sasha does not understand Jay's north of England sense of humour and some-times thinks she is being critical of her by some of the comments Jay makes. On one occasion Sasha becomes upset by Jay's comments about people who are religious. She is avoiding Jay at break time and is wondering whether she should leave the course as she feels Jay is having a go at her.

In the end Sasha speaks to the tutor about this who arranges a meeting with them both to discuss this. In the end it turns out that Sasha is projecting a lot of insecurities onto Jay. She feels insecure being a foreigner in England and not under-standing some of the cultural norms. She feels vulnerable as she knows Jay is gay and her background has involved strict religious and heterosexual norms.

She thinks Jay does not like her because she is heterosexual and a housewife conforming to social norms.

Jay is shocked by what is said. She never felt any strong feelings about Sasha who is a quiet member of the group. She acknowledges that sometimes she is brash and loud but a lot of this is insecurity as a lesbian woman, in a minority in the group and some of it is her dry northern humour. She never meant to cause harm to anyone.

Both of them have to assimilate what they have heard but at least having a dia-logue opens up what has been going on under the surface and means they can both continue in the group even if they don't become friends as such. Sasha starts to acknowledge for herself that she has been scared of Jay and some of this links to homophobic attitudes within her own family, growing up.

Trusting others/Daring to be open

In a small survey of a group of previous diploma students, I asked what the main challenges had been doing the self-awareness and personal development work on the Course. All the respondents identified some difficulty in opening up and talking about personal issues or past experiences:

The main challenges for me were about trusting other peers on the course with personal and possibly painful histories/memories which were important for self-awareness and self-development work. This was especially during PD (Personal Development) group work and activities with peers who you might not 'connect' with on a personal basis. I did not find personal therapy a challenge.

and:

I think initially the main challenge was opening up in front of people I didn't really know and a fear of saying something silly or irrelevant. I didn't fully understand how the PD group was supposed to work to begin with and it made me feel worried at getting it wrong.

and:

The challenge was in exposing vulnerable aspects of myself that I had hidden, even from myself, at times.

These all show the importance of course groups feeling safe enough for sharing to occur and people trusting other members of their group with personal information. Students identified that what helped this process was when other people were open, when they felt that they had a right to time and space in the group and:

building relationships with peers and recognising they were on the same journey as myself was empowering and aided the process.

So, there is a sense of everyone working together like a team towards the personal development goal.

Protective strategies

We all have protective strategies which we will use to keep ourselves safe. This may be a reluctance to revisit our pasts and the emotions which were linked with adverse experiences. Sometimes students are protecting themselves so much that they struggle to express real emotions or feel bad when they start to become emotional or become tearful.

Sometimes trainees are not aware of their defensive behaviour until they have started the therapy training and personal development work:

I realised, through attending personal therapy and the PD group, that I had built some strong defensive walls around myself. I explored, for example, in personal therapy, how some past colleagues had viewed me as scary. In discussing this, I recognised that my stressed state, in my final years as a teacher, had caused me to subconsciously protect myself, putting across a 'hard woman' image that was difficult for colleagues to penetrate. In the PD group I asked my peers what they thought, did I come across as scary? They were very surprised at this view of me and a number of them recognised that they too had used similar defence mechanisms. This prompted an insightful and powerful discussion. I was able to expose my vulnerability, in a safe space, where, not only were my feelings and thoughts valued and validated, but my revelations prompted others to expose aspects of their psyche that had been hidden. Building up trust with classmates and allowing myself to express feelings, I would normally hide, was liberating in ways I couldn't have imagined.

This is a powerful example of how the personal development work on a training course can help a person understand themselves more and enable them to become less defensive so that they could be more effective in their counselling work.

This is in contrast to the Mia case study in Chapter 9 where the student leaves the course feeling critical of the expectations and personal awareness requirements and, in particular, not being able to use feedback.

Conclusion

In this chapter, I have looked at a range of issues and challenges which may arise when you do a counselling or therapeutic training course. I have identified how this training is different from other forms of professional training with its particular personal demands. I have shared my experiences both as a student and as a trainer and drawn on some accounts from previous students who faced and worked through their challenges.

I hope this has given you a flavour as to the depth of personal development work which is required and has prepared you for the possible struggles you may encounter as you start to look at yourself and your past during your work on the course and in personal therapy.

References

Hawkins, P. and Shohet, R. (2012) *Supervision in the Helping Professions*. Maidenhead: OU Press.

Jung, C. (1991) *Aion: Research into the Phenomenology of Self (Collected Works of C. G. Jung)*. London: Routledge.

McBeath, A. (2019) The motivations of psychotherapists: An in-depth survey. *Counselling Psychotherapy Research*, 19, 377–387.

Mearns, D. and Thorne, B. (2011) *Person-Centred Counselling in Action*. London: Sage.

Chapter 5

The joys and challenges of diversity

Tara Fox and Jayne Godward

Introduction

This chapter will look at what a trainee brings to the counselling training with regards to their identity and how this will affect their relationships in the course group. We will explore diversity issues and intersectionality. The reader will be encouraged to explore their feelings around difference and look at the challenge of facing their own prejudices, stereotypes and fears. Case studies will be given of issues which have arisen in training groups and the authors will share their experiences of teaching about diversity and addressing issues of difference and intersectionality which have arisen.

In this chapter, we will help you to:

- examine what diversity is
- reflect on your personal heritage, identity and the importance of intersectionality
- prepare for working with diversity in your training group
- help you to consider the importance of being aware of prejudices and values that will impact the counselling relationship.

What do we mean?

Diversity is a term used so frequently that we would like to begin this chapter by examining the meaning of the word. From the 14th century word *diversite*, diversity means the 'quality of being diverse, fact of difference between two or more things or kinds; variety; separateness; that in which two or more things differ' (Online Etymology Dictionary, 2024).

During your training you will encounter many differences that are visible such as skin colour and gender for example as well as multiple opinions and life experiences which are largely unseen until people begin to speak openly with one another.

DOI: 10.4324/9781003405757-6

Sameness can be assumed when we see visible similarities just as difference in visible characteristics may lead to assumed difference of culture and opinions, values etc. Assumed sameness is problematic in that it prevents you from opening your experience to new information. Assuming differences can hold you back or make you wary of each other's opinions leading to fears of judgment.

This chapter aims to celebrate the diversity of the training group whilst recognising the sensitive nature of such conversations about difference.

The following activity is helpful for initiating respectful discussions about identity. It helps you to think of identity as a sense of self in relationship to others which is important in working with clients.

Identity

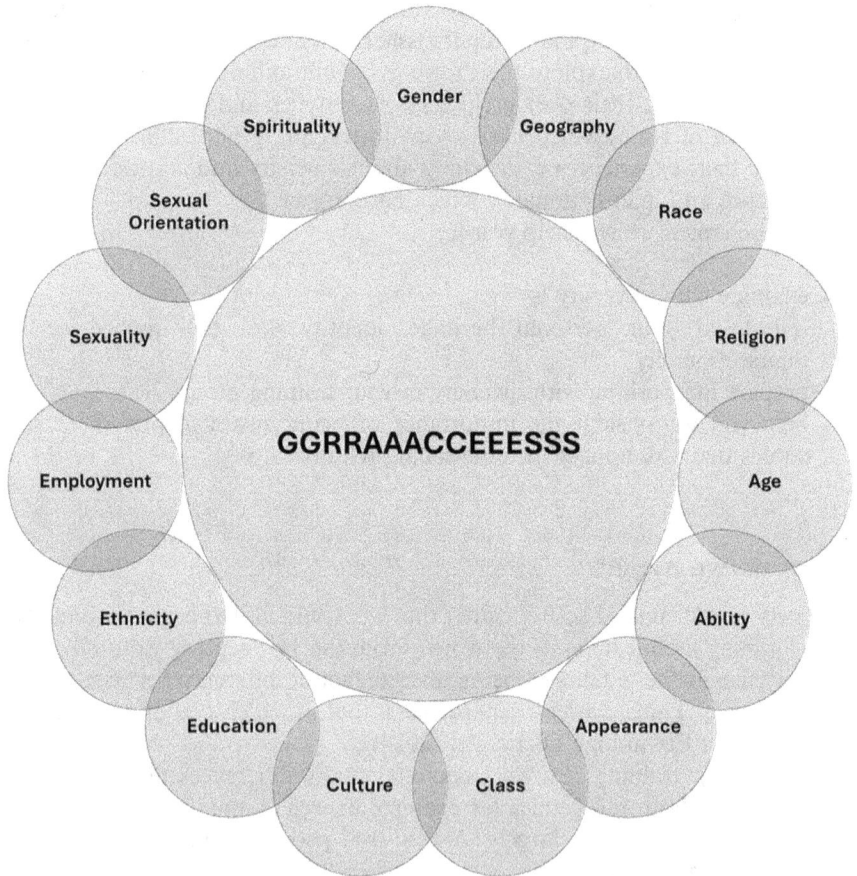

Figure 5.1 Social GGRRAAACCCEEESS

Consider your identity – the multiple identities that you have. I value the work of John Burham and colleagues who created the term Social GGRRAAACCEEESSS (Burnham, Alvis and Whitehouse, 2008). The acronym describes aspects of personal and social identity that have different levels of power and privilege.

Tara's multiple identities

Being a woman means I have a marginalised identity but as a white person I have privilege as I do not face racism in the community where I live. I have increased my socio-economic status through education and employment affording me further privileges. My spirituality is marginalised holding me back from speaking my true beliefs outside of my spiritual community, but my sexuality brings me privileges as I do not face discrimination for my heterosexuality. Some of these identities are visible and some are not. The ones that are not visible can be shared or held back depending on the context in which I am in.

Activity: Social GGRRAAACCEEESSS

Gender Geography Race Religion Age Ability Appearance Culture Class/caste Education Employment Ethnicity Spirituality Sexuality Sexual orientation.
  Consider your own identities and list them here:

- Which of your identities are privileges and give you power?
- Which ones are marginalised and subjugated?
- How is your view of yourself influenced by the Social GGRRAAACCEEESSS?

Visible and invisible aspects of identity

John Burnham (2012) offers a figure for how social GGRRAAACCEEESSS may be voiced or unvoiced and visible and invisible. This has been adapted for you to add your identities. On the next page I have added my visible identities to the circle. The ones on the outside are invisible and may be voiced or unvoiced.

You could pair up with someone on the course to co create a picture of your identities and how these are similar or different to each other. This would shift your unvoiced ones to the voiced area making them known to another. Only share what you feel safe to share and notice what this feels like to share the invisible and unvoiced parts of your identity with another.

Discussions about difference including power and oppression can be challenging to facilitate but the decision to avoid this is more than unhelpful and potentially damaging to members and the tutor alike.

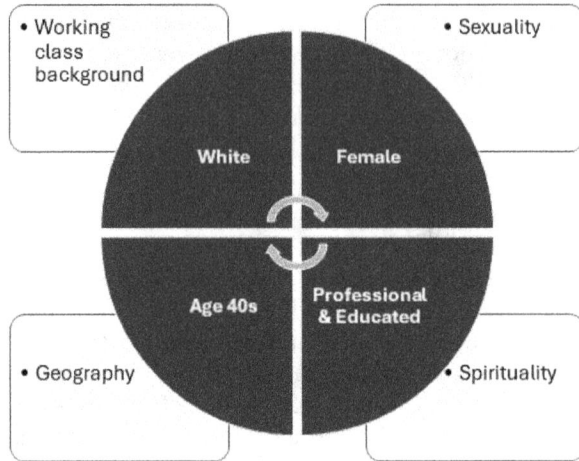

Visible and Invisible aspects of identity

Figure 5.2 Visible and invisible aspects of identity

Intersectionality

The intersecting identities in a course group along with the areas of privilege, domination and oppression contribute different lenses through which you see the world and each other. Multicultural counselling recognises how clients bring their multiple group identities into the therapy room and how these are different lenses in which people see and interpret the world they live in (Ivey, D'Andrea and Ivey 2012). Equally within counselling training groups the groups that people identify with need to be valued and respected by creating a space for these narratives to be heard.

The US has responded to the western theoretical orientations: humanistic, psychodynamic and cognitive behavioural by pioneering multicultural counselling and social justice approaches which have become fourth and fifth forces of counselling and psychotherapy (Ratts 2011). They recognise how social and cultural issues are central to people's lives rather than extra factors to consider. Similarly in the training group your social and cultural history affects the way in which you see the material delivered in class and informs your discussion contributions and emotional impact of the training.

Other people's views can be a strain to hear and to separate from one's own life stories. Developing compassion for others' differences as well as similarities aligns your personal development with the demands of client work.

The following activity is adapted from the Tree of Life groups which were created originally for the vulnerable children in east and south Africa and is now used as a tool to support people, groups and communities to share narratives and give meaning to experiences (Lock 2016). This narrative tool opens your mind and heart to re authoring your own story helping you to gain a stronger sense of your own identity.

Activity: Tree of Life (from Ncube 2006)

- Roots – draw your origins, your family, culture and heritage.
- Ground – This is your current place where you live and your current passions and interests.
- Branches – These are your hopes and future possibilities.
- Leaves – These are the special people in your life who support you now or have in the past. These can be people who are no longer alive.
- Fruits – These are the gifts you have received in life such as characteristics you have taken on board.

Engaging in this activity and hearing stories from the tree of life may help you to develop more compassion for yourself and for other people's narratives of the forest of their lives.

Working with diversity in training groups – Jayne's experience

One of the most rewarding and yet challenging aspects of my work as a trainer is addressing diversity issues within my teaching groups. This begins at pre-diploma level with the counselling certificate courses I work on and continues at Diploma level both undergraduate and post-graduate.

At Diploma or practitioner level students are normally required to look at diversity further but in terms of working with clients in the counselling relationship. They are expected to really challenge their beliefs and values and look at their fears and prejudices.

Ponder point

Why is it important for you to challenge your beliefs and values and examine your fears and prejudices prior to and whilst training to become a counsellor?

This is challenging work for the student and will be what you are expected to do to be effective in your work as a therapist, as if you did not look at your own personal baggage before you went to work with clients, there is a danger of you imposing your views on that person or there is a risk of you treating your clients less fairly due to your prejudices or the stereotypes you hold. You may say 'I am not prejudiced. I don't discriminate. I can work with all people.' I believe this is impossible.

Our society and the culture we grew up in will have instilled in us with certain views and attitudes towards others. We do not live in a value-free society. Despite the development of equal opportunities legislation and progress in terms of increased rights for minority groups, we live in a society which is racist, sexist, homophobic, ageist etc., where minority groups are still treated less well and where individuals suffer trauma due to unfair treatment and discrimination.

A lack of self-awareness means we could easily hold attitudes to clients or ourselves which are based on negative views and that we could offend or cause harm by what we say or by our unconscious bias, even if we did not have that intention.

Case study: Janice and Daren – Challenges to pre-conceived ideas

Janice is a white, middle-class, middle-aged counsellor. She has gone to work in a youth agency as a trainee counsellor. One of her first clients is a young black man aged 18. She has had a fairly sheltered life, growing up in a small village with little ethnic diversity. She imagined black youths to be associated with drugs and gangs and not working hard at school, due to media representation. Fortunately, she is aware that these are stereotypes as she enters the counselling room and also of her whiteness and the advantages, she has had in life due to this.

She is able to park some of her prejudices but cannot put aside her whiteness and middle-class and middle-aged appearance. In their first session rather than avoiding the obvious differences, Janice broaches the issues of difference and checks out if Daren is happy working with her. It turns out that Daren is from a middle-class family and is at University but is struggling with depression due to the high expectations of his family. His problems are far from the issues which Janice anticipated.

At first Daren is not sure if he will be able to relate to this woman who is a lot older than him, but she is from a similar background to his parents in terms of education and economic status and is rather like one of his helpful female white tutors at university, so he is hopeful.

This case study highlights how stereotypes in society could scupper a counselling relationship and how it is not just the counsellor who will judge the client, but the client will be judging the counsellor in terms of diversity.

Increased awareness of our attitudes to difference and diversity and our identity and differences in relation to others is essential and is usually addressed in the course group and course content.

Historically counselling courses were mainly attended by white, middle-class people, often, women who were from educated and economically comfortable backgrounds. When I did my training over 25 years ago, this was more the case. Now groups are more diverse as more people can access funding and awareness of mental health issues has increased. I find it exciting that students from different ethnic backgrounds and working-class people can now access training and that there is more diversity in terms of age, sexuality and gender.

We are all the same here ...

In the past it seemed easier for group members and tutors to just ignore the obvious differences in the room and to pretend everyone was the same. After all everyone is at the same starting point and have signed up, maybe paid and had the right entry qualifications to do a course. Haven't they? We are all the same and are all in it together?

Ponder points

Why can't differences in a course group be ignored?
Why can't everyone be treated the same in the group and in therapeutic work?

People starting a counselling course at any level are bringing their back-grounds and culture with them and cannot leave these at the door. If you think of the identities which Tara identified earlier, these are going to impact on our ability to relate to other people and may create barriers or make it easier to form relationships.

Often people have hidden needs which may mean they struggle with certain activities in class or may find it harder to relate to others, whilst others may find previous difficulties with other people due to racism, sexism, classism may prevent them sharing in the group or being themselves. There may be a real fear of being judged.

Case study: Sharon

Sharon is a white woman in her 40s. She has joined a counselling course in her local community centre. On the surface her group looks homogeneous. There are a lot of white faces and middle-aged women. There are only a couple of men in the group who are white.

She is nervous as she struggled at school and did not achieve many qualifications. She works in the local supermarket and has been attracted to counselling due to her struggles with mental health issues.

What emerges as the group starts to introduce itself is that there are a lot of dif-ferences between Sharon and the other group members. Most come from fairly middle-class occupations and want to develop counselling skills to enhance their work, e.g., teachers, social workers etc. and are reasonably well off, many have partners and children, obviously they are well educated and live in the leafy part of town.

Sharon has a strong local accent and does not feel articulate compared to her peers and she realises that this is going to be a barrier. She lives alone in a rented flat near the community centre with no printer at home and an unreliable internet connection.

Here there are several hidden differences which will not be apparent and treating everyone the same would mean Sharon will be at a disadvantage.

Some groups will have more obvious differences and on the higher-level courses e.g., Undergraduate or Post-graduate diploma, the tutor will normally encourage you to talk about your experience of feeling and being different and your fears in the group.

Fears around difference may include:

- I am the only person of colour here and I have suffered discrimination before and will not be accepted.
- I appear to be the only gay woman here – will I be accepted or seen as a threat by some?
- I have a strong faith. I am not going to disclose and be mocked for it.
- I am the youngest person in this group – they will think what do they know? Why are they here?
- I am the oldest member of the group – they will think I am too old to train and not capable of learning new things.
- I am the only man in the group – the women won't want to talk to me.
- I struggle with dyslexia – am I going to be able to cope with the work?
- I have ADHD and struggle to focus during lessons. Will I be able to manage?

If everyone were treated the same there would be no consideration for the emotional undercurrent which could be going on and learning and communication would be blocked. People would not get the support they needed from the tutor and group.

One way of addressing fears and anxieties is for a group contract to be drawn up which is usually underpinned by a wish for groups to be non-judgemental and have respect for difference and everyone's views. This can form part of a contract to help make things safer.

Authors like Arao and Clemens (2013) question the idea of 'safe spaces' in training for diversity and social justice. If safe means being free from harm or risk or avoiding difficulties and challenge, then there will not be open dialogue on diversity and differences and the injustices in society. Instead, they suggest that the aim should be to provide a 'brave space' where people do take risks and do engage truthfully with others. If your course group is too safe there may not be any learning taking place. People may be avoiding conflict and challenge instead. These authors quote a reminder of what learning involves:

learning necessarily involves not merely risk, but the pain of giving up a former condition in favour of a new way of seeing things.

(Arao & Clemens, 2013, p. 141)

Considering diversity and working with it

Diversity is complex because cultures are constantly changing and it is not possible to be culturally competent e.g., fully understand a culture and feel confident about it, as if you can say 'I've done that – I've worn the tee shirt'. We need to be alert and culturally sensitive, for example, what might have been OK for one person ten years ago may not be OK now and what might be OK for one person from a cultural background now may not be OK for a person from the same culture. We all need to be reviewing our approaches to others and attempt to work in a client-centred way to meet people's needs rather than presuming.

Terms used to describe a person from a minority group will keep changing and even if you are in a minority group you may not want to be labelled with that term or put under the same umbrella. It is best to ask people if you are unsure.

I am aware that it is easy for me to make mistakes and that I am constantly learning so I am empathic to my students who are also trying to grapple with these issues. The best plan is not to presume anything and to be curious. It is ok not to know. We need to understand what our client's culture means to them and what their experience is. It is about their needs not ours!

Challenges in the course group

The following activity invites you to consider the difficulties through the lens of diversity. Read through the scenario below and consider your reactions to this. There are three perspectives to consider including the student who is struggling, the tutor and the course group.

Case study: Saleema

Saleema a student with a Muslim heritage was hiding the decision she had made to not follow the Muslim faith. There were three other Muslim students in the group, and she feared they would judge her harshly. This was impacting on her sense of belonging in the group. Her assumptions about how she would be seen in the group also affected her emotionally and she was starting to arrive late to sessions and spoke less in the course group. The other students had noticed this and were concerned about her because she had previously been bubbly and spoke more when the course first started.

- What would you advise Saleema to do?
- What would you expect the tutor to do?
- What do you think the students could do to help Saleema?

There is no golden rule book for what anyone should do here, any student, group and tutor would find this challenging but discussions about prejudices, discrimination and fears are a regular part of good counselling training. Educators know that assumptions make an 'ass of you and me' and regular attention to difference in the room helps to confront hidden anxieties when managed respectfully by the course group and tutor.

The assumptions here might be that Saleema is a devout Muslim like her peers as she looks similar to them. Also, her behaviour may be misinterpreted.

Students can start to feel something is wrong and may decide to tackle this outside of the course group starting up conversations like 'Are you ok?' or 'I thought we got on well together have I done something to upset you?' These attempts to resolve the interpersonal issues usually make them worse as the student in this case study may feel singled out and 'othered' by the attention which could be interpreted by Saleema as 'I am different to the group' or 'I do not fit in here' or 'I am an outsider' or 'I am being a problem'. Instead of singling anyone out the tutor could address the group as a whole and invite people to share aspects of their identity to keep the discussion safely contained within a session. This would give Saleema a challenge to say what she chooses about her identity that is currently hidden.

The core conditions of empathy for each other, respect and genuineness can be modelled by the tutor who shows value for the uniqueness of each person. Care and compassion for each other can be cultivated through modelling by the tutor. Nell Noddings (2013) in her book *Caring: A Relational Approach to Ethics and Moral Education* advocates the cultivation of this in learning environments as a foundation for learning to take place.

In furtherance of this if we consider the values of the BACP (2018) too of 'appreciating the variety of human experience and culture', 'facilitating a sense of self that is meaningful to the person(s) concerned within their personal and cultural context' and 'respecting human rights and dignity' then we can see how these responsibilities are crucial in the course group.

Handling mistakes

Consider the following:

- A student calls her colleague 'she' when the person has made it clear that they want to be known as 'they'. The colleague becomes upset about this.
- A female student is worried about not being accepted by her white clients. Her colleague says 'you'll pass as Spanish with your skin colour'.
- A male student returns after being off sick, his female peers say 'was it man flu?'
- A student says to her peer 'Oh are you gay? You don't look it.'

- Alice has a strong regional accent and is proud of this and where she comes from. Her peer starts to imitate this in the group and Alice looks visibly upset but then laughs it off.

These comments are known as 'microaggressions' which can be defined as 'conscious and unconscious, direct and indirect insults, slights and discriminatory messages that, accumulated over time, can result in trauma' (Guest, 2019). Over time these comments leave a scar and start to affect our self-concept and our attitude towards our identity. A microaggression is like pricking a wound which is already there.

Limited research has been done into microaggressions in counselling, but it has been found that microaggressions related to race and gender in counselling indicate a cultural arrogance which will damage the working alliance with clients and will reduce the safety of the counselling relationship, thus affecting therapeutic progress (see Davis et al., 2016).

Some microaggressions are quite shocking to read and show a real lack of sensitivity and awareness in those who say these things. See Nadal (2014) for examples from a gay man's perspective.

If a microaggression happens in one of my groups, I would aim to challenge what has been said as it is not ok to let it pass. Often the recipient will laugh or brush it off, but the hurt will still be there. The person who made the statement may not even be aware they have said anything harmful and may have done so out of ignorance.

We can all make mistakes and say the wrong thing but, fitting with the duty of 'candour' within the BACP ethical framework (2018, p.7), we need to apologise and make amends to the other person.

Challenging prejudices and beliefs

Often the focus in training is on how we can work with clients from diverse backgrounds. Being in a group listening to the lived experiences of different members who have experienced discrimination and understanding their values and beliefs is priceless and hopefully, will expand your ability to empathise with others.

Having your own identity, values and beliefs does not cancel out someone else's different identity, values and beliefs. What we need to learn in groups is that you can hold one view whilst someone across the circle can hold another. So, for example, often in a course group there will be someone with a strong religious belief and opposite there will be someone, who is an atheist. Or there will be a person who is right wing in their politics sitting next to someone who is a socialist. Part of the learning is to accept the difference, even though this could be very challenging as normally you would mix or choose to mix with people with similar ideologies.

You will need to be able to tolerate different views and beliefs when you are working with clients but build a bridge to work together.

Often when we ask students what they might struggle with in others they are unable to say. They might say that they have done a lot of training in diversity and that they are used to working with a range of people. I tend to be a bit suspicious about this, because no matter how much training you have done, it is impossible to be value free and totally non-judgemental.

To survive as humans in an often, unsafe society, we have to make judgements, and we feel safer with people who seem to have similar identities to ourselves. We are all prejudiced and we all discriminate. We need to do this to survive.

Activity: The last train home

It is late at night, and you have just boarded a quiet train. Who are you most likely to you sit near and who would you avoid of these people:

- The young white woman in high heels on her way home from a night out
- The older Muslim woman who has just been waved off by her daughter
- The older white man returning from a night out with his mates
- The black twenty-year-old playing with his phone on his way home from work
- The white youth who is fidgeting and talking to himself after being seen off by his girlfriend

Who you would decide to sit next to would depend on your own identity, life experience, values and beliefs and, of course, prejudices.

Similarly for clients they may feel more comfortable working with someone who has similarities to themselves or who seems 'safe' within their experience.

There has been some interesting research into the differences in race between client and counsellors and the white client's reaction to Black and Asian Minority Ethnic (BAME[1]) counsellors. Here the BAME counsellor's had different reactions from their white counsellor. One person said that they felt they had to justify themselves a bit and needed to prove themselves more because they thought the person may be thinking 'Is this person competent?' (Spalding, Grove and Rolfe, 2018).

It is really important to be aware of who you are and what you are bringing to the counselling relationship by exploring your identity, values and beliefs on the training course, can help you understand your identity but also how that might impact on your clients.

Your individual characteristics will give you more or less advantage in the eyes of your client. If your client has struggled in their lives with people in positions of authority, they may already ascribe some authority to you 'the counsellor' and see you as another 'health professional' As a counsellor normally you would be aiming to create as equal relationship as possible, but your client may put you on a pedestal or be disparaging even before you start your work together.

Case study: Shaun

Shaun has recently been diagnosed with autism. He is now in his early thirties but most of his life has been a battle to gain a diagnosis and have his neurodiversity recognised. He has often been in an 'us and them' situation with the professionals in his life who have expected him to behave in a certain way. This included teachers, social workers and mental health practitioners. People did not understand why he could not conform and why he struggled in school and college and later work. He has become angry and disillusioned with society and is suffering from depression. He is coming to see a counsellor at a specialist autism service but is not feeling hopeful as most of his experiences of professionals have been negative.

As you can see here, that even before you enter the counselling room with Shaun, he will have certain prejudices and stereotypes about professionals especially those who are neurotypical and may be expecting a negative outcome. There will be barriers to break down here even if you are experienced and understanding of neurodiversity. Your first step may be to allow space for Shaun to talk about his fears and concerns and be empathic to these. Acknowledging differences here will be important.

Conclusion

This chapter has encouraged you to explore issues of difference and to reflect on your own identity. We hope this has helped you to develop more compassion for yourself as you grapple to work with diversity and has made you curious about the different experiences of people in your training group who bring their unique way of being and experiencing into the group. It is hoped that you can see more of how intersectionality and power interact and can reinforce prejudices and stereotypes which we are better to know about than to deny. This chapter has been challenging and inspiring to write and has aimed to promote deeper thinking around how your training group can help you have discourse about difference in a way that is respectful, compassionate and empowering.

Note

1 This term was being used at the time of the study.

References

Arao, B. and Clemens, K. (2013) From safe space to brave spaces. In Landreman, L. M. (Ed.), *The Art of Effective Facilitation*. New York: Stylus Publishing LLC.

Burnham, J. (2012) Developments in the social GGRRAAACCEEESSS: Visible-invisible and voiced-unvoiced. In Krause, I. (Ed.), *Culture and Reflexivity in Systemic Psychotherapy: Mutual Perspectives.* London: Karnac.

Burnham, J., Alvis, D., and Whitehouse, L. (2008) Learning as a context for differences and differences as a context for learning. *Journal of Family Therapy*, 30(4), 529–542.

BACP (2018) Ethical Framework for the Counselling Professions. Available from www.bacp.co.uk/events-and-resources/ethics-and-standards/ethical-framework-for-the-counselling-professions/ [date accessed 18 October, 2023].

Davis, D.E., DeBlaere, C., Brubaker, K., Owen, J., Jordan, T. A. II, Hook, J. N., and Van Tongeren, D. R. (2016) Microaggressions and perceptions of cultural humility in counselling. *Journal of Counselling and Development*, 94(4), 483–493.

Online Etymology Dictionary (2024) Diversity (n.). Available from www.etymonline.com/word/diversity [date accessed 28 February, 2024].

Guest, Y. (2019) Between black and white. *Therapy Today*, 30(3), 26–29.

Ivey, A. E., D'Andrea, J. M., and Ivey, M. B. (2012). *Theories of Counseling and Psychotherapy: A Multicultural Perspective.* Sage Publications.

Lock, S. (2016) The Tree of Life: A review of the collective narrative approach. *Educational Psychology Research & Practice*, 2(1), 2–20.

Ncube, N. (2006) The Tree of Life Project: Using narrative ideas in work with vulnerable children in Southern Africa. *International Journal of Narrative Therapy and Community Work*, 1, 3–16.

Nadal, K. L. (2014) Stop saying "That's so gay!": 6 types of microaggressions that harm LGBT people. Available from https://psychologybenefits.org/2014/02/07/anti-lgbt-microaggressions [date accessed 28 February, 2024].

Noddings, N. (2013) *Caring: A Relational Approach to Ethics & Moral Education*, 2nd edn updated. Berkeley: University of California Press.

Ratts, M. J. (2011) Social justice counseling: Toward the development of a fifth force among counseling paradigms. *The Journal of Humanistic Counselling Education and Development*, 48(2), 160–172.

Spalding, B., Grove, J., and Rolfe, A. (2018) An exploration of Black, Asian and Minority Ethnic counsellors' experiences of working with White clients. *Counselling Psychotherapy Research Journal*, 19, 75–82.

Chapter 6

The impact of training on self and others

Tara Fox

In this book, we are looking at the impact of training on yourself across various chapters. Doing counselling training is sometimes referred to jokingly as the 'divorce course.' In this chapter, I will aim to look at how far this is true as my focus will be on the effects on personal relationships, by referring to research into the effects on partner relationships.

The impact of training from partners' perspectives is a new area of research I am examining and the findings from this research thus far are presented and discussed.

This chapter looks at:

- personal relationships from trainee perspectives
- the experiences of partners
- pilot study research; initial findings.

Personal relationships: Trainee perspectives

Knowing about the impact on personal relationships can help you to make choices in line with your expectations from an informed position. During training, you will learn more about boundaries and personal safety and this is a game changer for trainees, some of whom may never have considered these issues before in any depth. This is likely to impact relationships especially those where you have been inclined to overstep your boundaries by offering more than you are typically comfortable to give. As you develop more awareness of self-care you may decide you don't want to go along with others' plans and become more questioning of others' motivations and intentions. Your availability is certainly going to be affected. The boundary of the counselling sessions means you are not available on the phone for example and may therefore not be available to respond to partners. This can feel like a sudden change partners may not be used to.

Similarly, when you are in personal therapy or supervision you are simply unavailable. Being unavailable may be something new for you and your relationship and therefore create tensions. Creating safe and confidential spaces

DOI: 10.4324/9781003405757-7

for clients can impact the availability of your mind too. There are aspects of your work you are unable to share with loved ones and this can be something different. It can feel strange to have aspects of your life that cannot be shared with your partner, and you may feel as though this is not OK. Again, this relates to boundaries and knowing you can still have closeness without telling your partner every aspect of your work.

Equally, your new activities are exciting and rewarding and you will begin to feel more confident in yourself. It can be wonderful to share this new confidence with your partner and you may wish to engage in new activities together. Positive experiences in group work can increase your self-esteem. As you experience acceptance from your peers you may also begin to accept yourself. As your self-worth and emotional security increase, it is inevitable that this will impact your relationship.

A literature review about self-esteem and romantic relationship quality evidenced that high self-esteem can improve relationship quality (Erol and Orth, 2016). When you feel safe and accepted with your peers during training encounters this can bring confidence in trying new things out including how you communicate with loved ones. This was found in a study with counselling trainees by Robson and Robson (2008) where student safety in PD groups was essential for taking risks and trying new things.

I recall as my own confidence increased through training and working with clients, I felt more able to take on new activities such as paragliding over the sea and taking skate lessons with my partner. I also felt more confident in going to fancy restaurants and wearing different clothes. My communication about my own needs became more clearly communicated and my partner appreciated my honesty and more genuine approach to decision making. This has been found in a recent study with five participants who had all completed their training within 18 months. Training gave them all permission to change bringing a 'sense of relief and liberation' (Daldorph and Hill, 2022). As you begin to communicate with authenticity there can be a sense of freedom from fears to speak your truth.

Learning about new theories and assimilating this new knowledge leads to questioning oneself and those around us, your worldview widens as there is more available to see.

In Chapter 4, more is suggested about the vulnerability of trainee therapists and here I would like to revisit the self-doubt aspect that naturally arises through training, and you may need more reassurance from your partner hoping they can support you through this self-questioning.

Past traumas unexplored will need to be processed in therapy and you may feel torn between sharing your pain with your partner and protecting them from the suffering you may be going through.

Building a counsellor self is a new part of your identity and generally involves developing your genuineness. Being truer to yourself can be challenging as it can lead to making changes in your life. Changing friendship groups for example, jobs, and commitments. It most certainly supports you in being more honest with others but not all relationships can cope with frank conversations.

Ponder points

Are there some people in your life you wish to be more authentic with?
Are there some people who would not appreciate this and therefore could be harmful to the relationship?

Some patterns of relating are hard to change and some people are too vulnerable to engage with authentically. Some relationships do not require you to be authentic anyway due to the expectations of the role, for example, at work you may bracket off your true feelings about your colleagues or manager. Our parents have related to us in a certain way throughout our lives and you may find this the most challenging of relationships in which to be genuine.

Many of our friendships still work well for us even though we don't show our authentic selves. You may go swimming with a friend every week, but they don't need to know how you truly feel about your life. Working all this out can feel complex. Especially when the BACP (2018, pp. 10–11) state how practitioners need to develop 'candour,' 'sincerity' and be 'trustworthy' and the core condition of congruence lends itself to speaking more of your truth.

Choosing to train as a counsellor has been described by Daldorph and Hill (2022, p. 72) as an 'unconscious act of self-care: a promise of self-discovery and permission to change how they relate to themselves and others.'

I have reflected on this and consider that intentionality plays a part in the impact of training on self and others.

Activity

Reflecting on my relationship with myself and others ...

- What is my intention for my relationships?
- What is my intention for my relationship with myself?
- What might be my hidden intentions for my relationship with myself and others?

The following case shows how our intentions for our relationship with ourselves and others are present and bring about changes throughout training:

Case study: Mark

Mark began counselling training bringing a history of difficulties with ex-partners. He finds closeness hard, and his current partner of two years is demanding more of him. Mark brings an intention to be more open with his partner and to trust her more. He wants to feel more confident and less wary of being let down. His mum and dad were divorced when he was 10 and he felt in the middle and had to be strong keeping his feelings hidden to keep his dad happy. His hidden intention is to work with the client's vulnerability to appreciate his own and to effect change in other people's lives that he could not influence as a child.

How might Mark's intentions affect his current relationship?
What do you imagine might be challenging?
What might the positives be for his relationship?

Often, we find it hard to access our hidden intentions as this unfolds over time and with increased self-awareness and getting in touch with our vulnerabilities.

Experiences of partners

If you have a partner, they will hear the experiences you share with them and witness the impact of training on your behaviour. The influx of new theories takes time to process and self-questioning when shared with partners can tie you both in knots looking for reasons why, how and when. This soul searching can bring you closer together but equally, it challenges the equilibrium causing some anxiety. My partner felt as though he wanted to protect me from the cruel acts in the world and all I seemed to talk about was theories of personality development and unconscious processes. I was often analysing and had to set boundaries with myself to put this type of thinking down. I was also not available at set times because of client work, supervision or personal therapy.

Partners have to adjust their expectations of your flexibility and refresh their routines to accommodate this change.

When you are respecting confidentiality for your work this change can feel as though you are keeping things a secret and in extreme cases may develop a mistrust of your activities. It helps partners to understand that confidentiality does not mean keeping secrets but honouring the trust placed in you to fulfil the role. It is fine to say you are working with clients affected by childhood trauma or abuse issues as this is not a breach of confidence but informs them that you are working intensely and may need some quiet time for processing and more self-care.

Your partners may notice you becoming distracted and it can prevent undue concern if you can offer a reason for this and reassurance.

More positively your increased confidence can be lovely for partners to see giving your relationship a positive update. My partner enjoyed my slightly reserved nature extending to trying out different things and he needed to spend less time reassuring me or bigging me up to be brave with ongoing challenges in my work.

Pilot study: Focus group findings

Partners were invited to a focus group to share their experience of professional counselling training. This is the first of a range of groups planned to build up a bigger picture of partners' experiences. It was important that therapist partners had recently undergone training (up to two years qualified) so that participants could remember more of the impact training had on their relationship. Their identities were kept confidential, data anonymised, and consent obtained. Thematic analysis was used to find emerging themes

The questions asked were:

- What impact did therapy training have on your relationship?
- What challenges did you experience along the way as a result of this?
- How did you manage to overcome these?
- What were the positives for your relationship?
- Is there anything professional counselling training providers could do better to prepare or support trainees for the impact courses could have on their relationships?

Hearing partners' views was a humbling experience. I could see how these partners had adjusted their expectations of their romantic partner to allow time for them to study, attend therapy, supervision and placement. They saw the busyness of their partners as an opportunity to do more of the things they loved to do. One partner explained

I can amuse myself … ooh, I can crack on with that!

Equally, the training requirements were seen as contributing positive differences to the couple's planned activities. Another partner shared:

I gave her a lift to see her therapist and waited in the pub reading my book … afterwards, we would talk it through.

Partners were supportive of the emotional challenges of training and were a strong source of reassurance along the way being a listening ear and a witness to their suffering.

One partner explained:

he was preoccupied a lot … always thinking and found it hard to switch off.

Equally partners enjoyed witnessing the positive impact of training such as the joy of helping clients, taking less blame for difficult relationships with parents, using improved communication to share feelings, and showing more empathy for each other. The main problem for partners in this first group was the financial burden training placed on their relationship but in this case, the couples had managed to shoulder the strain, but were left wondering how essential books and resources could be shared across groups One said:

> He bought loads of books. Deliveries arrived every week.

They also expressed how training providers could explain to students how essential it is to open up to partners about what they are studying and how they are being impacted by the topics. This indicates how partners may feel in the dark about what they are going through and potentially this could cause confusion and worry.

The findings from this first group show how partners wish they were more involved in the subject areas being covered. One male partner explained how a timeline would help to plot the journey indicating how much therapy training and homelife are interlinked. The student brings the content home with them and partners felt that they needed advice about how to best support them during times of increased self-reflection and rumination. A partner explained:

> Don't forget you're not going through this alone. Please share what you are doing.

These initial findings show the impact of training on partners shedding a light on hidden aspects of the process of becoming a counsellor. I aim to continue this research so as to better support trainees and recognise the relational strain and shift in support needed at home.

Although this chapter has focused on the impact on partners, I appreciate the effect training may have on all relationships including friendships and family relationships. Professional counselling training often helps us to see the vulnerability in our parents and increase compassion for those with live with. Children of trainees is another area that could be explored. My children have only ever known me as a counsellor mum and have appreciated my knowledge of mental health and wellbeing but at times I have found it hard to respond just as a mum but as a counsellor mum. I have been guilty of analysing problems using psychological theory instead of just being a parent. My kids prefer me as a mum, not an analytical mentor.

Conclusion

This chapter intended to provide food for thought to help you to choose the best time to train as a therapist from more of an informed position. It has examined how doing counselling training can affect the person's relationships, in particular, with their spouse or partner and looked at ways this can be navigated. I hope that the issues raised here can help you to speak with your partner, if you are in a relationship and support your ongoing discussions. Something will inevitably need to be renegotiated between you both to adjust and allow for any changes but talking these through helps a great deal and does not need to result in 'the divorce course' scenario as is rumoured on the grapevine.

References

BACP (2018) *Ethical Framework for Good Practice for the Professions.* [Available from] www.bacp.co.uk/events-and-resources/ethics-and-standards/ethical-framework-for-the-counselling-professions/ [date accessed 9 January, 2025].

Daldorph, A. and Hill, S. (2022) The perceived impact of counselling training on students' personal relationships. *Counselling & Psychotherapy Research*, 24, 63–74.

Erol, R. and Orth, U. (2016) Self-esteem and the quality of romantic relationships. *European Psychologist*, 21, 274–283.

Robson, M. and Robson, J. (2008) Explorations of participants' experiences of a personal development group held as part of a counselling psychology training group: Is it safe in here? *Counselling Psychology Quarterly*, 21, 371–382.

Chapter 7

What kind of counsellor do you want to be?

Jayne Godward

Introduction

There are many approaches to counselling and different types of training leading to becoming a qualified counsellor or therapist. It is important that you choose the best course for you and are aware of how these programmes differ. This will usually depend on your philosophy of life and your view of human beings. Your course will need to match your personality and how you prefer to learn.

This chapter aims to help you look at the main aspects to consider and at some of the models of counselling that are offered on courses.

I will outline some of the main theoretical models underpinning counselling and psychotherapy qualifications including Person-Centred, Psychodynamic, Integrative and Relational.

There will be accounts from therapists who have done different types of training to help you examine why they chose these and the process involved.

So, in this chapter I will:

- introduce the main factors to consider when choosing a training programme
- share my own experiences of this process
- look at the commitment required to do counsellor training
- examine where and what to study
- give an overview of some the main models of counselling and therapy
- check out your personal beliefs about helping others linked to the above
- offer three accounts from different therapists about why they chose their training pathways.

Introducing the factors to consider

In my experience these are the factors which people consider when choosing a course, see the box below:

DOI: 10.4324/9781003405757-8

Training considerations

- Location
- Time and Day
- Cost
- Is funding available?
- Modality – theoretical approach being taught
- Type of training – is it very academic and more practice based?
- Placement, supervision and personal therapy requirements
- Components – what emphasis is placed on personal development as opposed to academic work? I.e., What are the different components of the training?
- Time/ Work commitment required

Many of these are practical considerations whilst others are more about the content and delivery of the course. To demonstrate this, I will talk about my own experience of how I chose my training programme in the section below.

Why I chose my own training

Location: When I decided to train to become a counsellor, I had already done a couple of counselling certificate courses locally but chose to look outside my area so that there would be less chance of meeting students I had taught as I was working in a college at the time. I chose to do a two-hour journey to another city to study.

Cost: The courses I considered had comparable costs with no student funding available but all within my budget. Most were afternoon and evening courses which was ok for me as I was able to take a day off work per week.

Modality/Approach: I was drawn to the person-centred approach as student-centred learning had been incorporated in my teaching since beginning work as a tutor. This was the idea that everyone has the potential to learn and grow and that we need to harness this potential and build on what people have already. So person-centred theory fit with my personal philosophy, values and beliefs.

Type of Training: Three courses were offering the same approach but one followed a stricter model and I felt this might be too rigid for me. The other felt less rigid but I did not feel it would be academic enough or rigorous enough for me, having come from an educational background.

Components: I settled on a university course which had different elements but included a lot of groupwork. This included community groups, personal development groups, skills groups and theoretical and practice input. Funnily enough and not surprising this is the model I still use when training students now as it feels effective.

Time: The day was 1–9 p.m. with breaks and a variety of activities and groups during that time. The journey there and back was used to read and reflect which suited me.

The course also included a residential each year of a weekend. This was personally challenging but also a good way of people really getting to know each other and gave us an opportunity for doing some in-depth personal development work.

Placement/supervision and therapy requirements: To complete the course, we had to do 144 hours of counselling practice and attend regular supervision. Twenty hours of therapy was also required.

(Normally a commitment of 100 hours placement and 20 hours of therapy seems to be common on most courses.)

Where to study? What kind of course?

I work with students on counselling certificate courses who have to decide what kind of course to go on after their training with me. Usually, the options consist of private training providers, FE colleges and Universities. There are advantages and disadvantages with all of these. Private training courses in smaller organisations usually offer smaller group sizes and more personalised training but may not have the facilities that colleges and universities can offer like access to library resources, recording facilities and a range of tutors.

The big bonus with college and university courses is that there is normally the facility of being able to get a student loan which students at smaller organisations can't access because the organisation's annual turnover may not be sufficient to meet government requirements.

You also need to decide whether you want an undergraduate type of course or a post-graduate course depending on if you have a degree already.

Here you will be deciding whether you want a course that is more academic or more practice based. Some students who already have higher qualifications and professional qualifications, choose to take a more practical Level 4 or undergraduate course rather than having to do in depth assignments and research. You need to decide what suits you.

From my experience training students so far, the academic level of counsellor training does not determine how successful you are as a counsellor later, it is more about the type of person you are and your previous experience that matters.

Some students do an undergraduate type of diploma and then do further training up to master's level and beyond as part of their continuing professional development.

What to study?

Although all courses should contain certain components with regards to professional practice, personal development, skills practice and theory. You need to check out how much time is taken on each element and whether your intended course looks rigorous enough. Is there enough skills training? Will you be regularly observed by tutors as well as peers? Is there proper professional practice training on elements you need to be able to work safely and in a beneficial way as a therapist – e.g., ethical practice, working within a legal framework, using professional skills, understanding the counselling role and the counselling relationship and very important, understanding and working with diversity.

What theoretical approach should you study?

There are many different approaches to counselling, and it is important that you choose a theoretical model which will suit who you are and your philosophy on life and what you think is helpful to people. This book is not a theory book but, in this section, I will touch briefly on some of the main modalities which you could train in, this being dependent on the cost and availability of this type of course in your area.

There are three main forces in psychology whose ideas underpin the approaches to counselling:

- Psychoanalysis
- Behavioural psychology
- Humanistic Psychology

From these evolved some of the current approaches to counselling. As I write this, I am very aware that these theories were originated by white, middle-class western males and were influenced by the culture of the people who developed these. Counselling is constantly evolving and other influences like multicultural and transpersonal perspectives are having some impact on the work we do as counsellors and therapists, but the basic approaches remain in terms of types of initial practitioner training offered. So, we will focus on these as a starting point for you to think about what kind of therapist you want to be.

The psychodynamic approach

This grew out of the work of Sigmund Freud. Here the focus is on unconscious motivation, innate drives, childhood experience and current behaviour and also how we use defence mechanisms in our lives (see Hough, 2021, pp. 83–86).

There is an emphasis on the past and how this affects us in the present and on how we protect ourselves internally from unpleasant experiences (defence mechanisms). Psychodynamic practitioners are interested in hidden or unconscious factors which affect our behaviour. There is an interest in relational dynamics and how past experiences affect current relationships. In this book we talk about transference and countertransference which are psycho-dynamic ideas which we need to be aware of when working with clients. This is where the client reacts to the therapist as if they were someone they knew or know in a different context (transference). The therapist can then react in response (countertransference).

There are some counselling diploma courses which focus specifically on the psychodynamic approach but in my experience, this is often included in Integrative courses which merge a few modalities together. You can choose to specialise and train to be a psychodynamic psychotherapist, but this will be a longer (usually four years) and more intense training requiring regular personal psychotherapy throughout the course.

The behavioural/cognitive behavioural approach

This model emerged from the work of a number of psychologists. The focus is on observing human behaviour and the reasons for this. They were interested in how behaviours are reinforced throughout life. Important figures were Pavlov (do you remember his dogs?), Watson and Skinner. Human behaviour is seen as a collection of learned behaviours. There is a big focus on rewards and punishments. Therapists aim to understand how problem behaviours are reinforced so that they can offer techniques to change these.

Unlike the psychodynamic approach, these practitioners are not interested in the unconscious mind or things that cannot be observed.

From the earlier behavioural psychology, cognitive behavioural therapy (CBT) has been developed and has grown in popularity and is an approved treatment in the NHS. This approach is interested in a person's thinking and how that affects their behaviour, so it goes beyond just looking at learned behaviours.

Some integrative courses include some training in CBT but often students who are interested in this area do their counselling or psychotherapy training first and then do CBT training as part of their continuing professional development. This may involve short courses of a few days or a proper certificate which might be a year in length part-time.

The person-centred approach

This approach is very different from the last two as there is an emphasis on the potential of each human being and a belief that people naturally want to grow and develop (self-actualise). Each individual is seen as unique and the important thing to understand is the person's experience and how they see the world. The founding theorists are Carl Rogers and Abraham Maslow.

A key difference is that generally the person-centred approach (PCA) does not rely on techniques and stresses the importance of the therapeutic relationship and the provision of the right conditions so that the client can reach their potential and discover their real self.

The therapists aim to understand a person's behaviour from the client's point of view (known as phenomenology) and do not offer an expert interpretation of this or look at it objectively from an external standpoint.

Courses with person-centred theory as a foundation vary from those which are purist and extremely student centred and very experiential to those which have the PC Approach as the main model but teach other theoretical ideas and are less experiential.

Integrative approaches

Some training organisations have developed their own integrative courses which incorporate several different theories. They will explain their rationale to you when you apply or whilst you are studying with them. For example, the course Tara teaches on follows a relational model which incorporates aspects such as person-centred, psychodynamic, cognitive behavioural therapy, transactional analysis (see below) etc. but the focus is on the creation and maintenance of the therapeutic relationship.

Many courses take on board research into the therapeutic relationship which has shown this is key to positive therapy outcomes and that success is less to do with who are and your approach and more to do with how you related to your clients, but they differ in the therapeutic tools they teach students and in some of the underpinning aspects of theory (see Reeves, 2022 for a discussion about integrative approaches and Cooper, 2008; Norcross, 2002).

Below I will briefly look at two specific models which are classified as being integrative (Short and Thomas, 2015), which you could study to become a therapist without having done previous practitioner training, although some of my previous students have specialised in these following therapeutic diplomas.

Gestalt Therapy

This sits within the humanistic approach but has its foundation in the psychodynamic approach. It incorporates aspects of person-centred, psychoanalysis and existentialism.

There is a focus on increasing self-awareness, awareness of others and of the environment. 'Here and now' experiencing is seen as creating greater choice and the client is encouraged to deal with unfinished business in the present. People are encouraged to take responsibility for themselves and be able to ask for what they want and to be able help others (see Short and Thomas, 2015, pp. 292–293).

Courses vary and may be a two-year diploma to become a counsellor or a longer more in-depth training to become a Gestalt psychotherapist.

Transactional Analysis

Again, this is grounded in the humanistic and psychodynamic approaches and integrates some person-centred and psychoanalytic ideas. Unlike psychoanalysis there is more focus on relationships and interactions between people rather than unconscious drives. In this therapy simple terms are used to explain processes and interactions which clients can understand. It includes a model of personality called the PAC, Parent, Adult, Child model and ideas on interactions known as transactions or strokes, games (looking at relational patterns) and other aspects looking at life patterns etc. (see Short and Thomas, 2015, Chapter 6).

Often students already on diploma courses dabble in this and do short training courses but some people decide to train fully in this approach and do psychotherapy training which may be four years, part-time.

Hopefully this section on different approaches in training has offered you a flavour as to what is on offer and will help you to consider what might suit you. It might be useful to ask yourself what you believe in terms of helping people. Here is a quiz to help with this process.

Personal beliefs quiz

What do you really believe about people and how they can be helped? For each of these decide whether you would answer – true or false.

1   The past and our early childhood always affects you throughout your life.
2   The counsellor needs to be adaptable and alter their approach according to the needs of the client.
3   Our early attachments affect the way we go on to relate to others and form relationships.
4   Some people cannot be helped by therapy.
5   People see what they want to see and have their own realities as we are all unique.
6   Therapy is about gaining a level of self-acceptance and coming to understand who you really are.
7   People need the help of expert therapists who can interpret what is going on.
8   As a counsellor you need to have a range of techniques and interventions at your disposal.
9   Just talking in a supportive, non-judgemental and empathic environment is enough to help a person change.
10   The way we think about a situation affects how we react emotionally.
11   People are often irrational in their thinking and beliefs and need to change these in order to be helped.
12   We are driven by unconscious motives and desires to act in certain ways.

13 People learn to behave in certain ways and are generally conditioned to be who they are.

14 People are basically good and have an innate potential for growth and development.

15 The therapeutic relationship is the crucial element in effective counselling.

See the end of this chapter for an assessment of these answers and the possible approach you are leaning towards.

I would strongly recommend reading up about different theoretical approaches before deciding which type of training to take. The following authors offer accessible texts to these if you are new to this area. (Hough, 2021; Reeves, 2022; Sanders, Williams and Rogers, 2021; Short and Thomas, 2015.)

Why therapists chose their courses?

In this next section I asked a range of experienced therapists why they chose the course they did and how it fit with their personal philosophy of life on how people could be helped. I also asked what the training involved linked to the theoretical approach they had chosen. There are some explanations of terms used in the foot notes I make after the accounts.

Couples counsellor

Reasons for choosing the course

I wanted to train as a couple therapist because I believed in Relate as an organisation. I respected the long history of Relate which used to be called Marriage Guidance Counselling. My own parents had divorced when I was in my teens, and I was left with a lot of questions about relationships and felt unsure about what a healthy relationship looked like. I had come out of an unhealthy one and therefore had much to learn.

Relate's approach to relationships fitted with my first-degree subject of psychology where we had looked at developmental theories such as Freud, Erikson and Bowlby. I had an analytical mind and therefore the power of the unconscious appealed to my natural curiosity about the hidden meaning of life. It also complimented my spirituality which centres on the belief in connection and the healing power of connection to self, others and spirit. I also valued the systemic approach[1] to understanding family dynamics and the function of a presenting issue for example how an affair can happen to encourage couples to work together and confront deeper relational issues.

Genogram work[2] was a useful tool for exploring intergenerational issues and 'couple fit.' I appreciated how I could help couples to connect or respectfully part their ways. I became more assertive through teaching communication skills with clients and learnt how to deconstruct an argument and am no longer fearful of conflict situations.

What the training involved

The training was relational psychodynamic and systemic. Psychodynamic approaches – object relations[3] for couple styles of relating and splitting, attachment theory for approaches to arguments and ways of showing love, Erikson for reflecting on missed life stages,[4] Freud for his defence mechanisms and personality development, transferences. Systemic approaches – for example, genogram work.

Integrative psychotherapist

Reasons for choosing the course

I decided to train to become a psychotherapist in 1989 just after my mother died from cancer. It was a very distressing time for me and my GP referred me to an NHS Psychodynamic Art Psychotherapist. I was clear that I didn't want to do any artwork and wanted to use the space to talk about my coping strategies which my therapist allowed me to do. Through this experience I learnt about my attachment patterns and my relationship with my mother. I was reading deeply around this time and decided to do an Integrative course in psychotherapy.

I studied at an innovative training centre in North London and worked with some eminent psychotherapists from the Humanistic and Psychodynamic traditions who influence the way I work today. The director of the training institute had an interest in subatomic physics and that was the basis and the philosophy underpinning the course. In basic terms the theory is that we relate to each other through wave functions, we attract and repel each other. In terms of energy some people radiate light and happiness and others heaviness and despair. Some people take up more density and space than others. There is a heaviness about them and others are more fluid and ethereal. The connectedness with self and interconnectedness with others was the core theme interspersed throughout the training.

What the training involved

The course had four dominant strands running throughout the three years of training. The first was Humanistic with the emphasis on the 'person to person' relationship. We studied modules on the Humanistic approach which included the work of Carl Rogers, Fritz Perls on Gestalt theory and Eric Berne on Transactional Analysis. This also covered the Existential and Phenomenological underpinnings where we looked at the work of the Existentialists, primarily, Martin Buber, Rollo May, Edmund Husserl and Irving Yalom.

Significantly attention was given to the second strand of study on the Psychodynamic Approach where we focused on the work of Sigmund Freud and Object Relations theorists, predominantly Donald Winnicott, Ronald Fairbairn, Harry Guntrip and Melanie Klein.

The third strand, which was quite unique at the time, was focus on the body. Using Einsteinian theory of light and energy we focused on and experimented with bodily mass and space. There was an integration of Attachment theory, growth and developmental change and Neuroscience with particular attention given to the emotional experience and energy.

The fourth strand was on the Transpersonal where we focused on Eastern and Western philosophies and the work of Carl Jung, Ken Wilber and Stanislaus Grof. This also encompassed the social and political environment.

We also had supervision practice and experiential groups for personal development. In addition, there were a number of weekend workshops where we would focus on themed activities connected to the course. Some of these were Rebirthing, Trauma, Gestalt work, Psychodrama and Mental Health. The emphasis was always on the experiential with a theoretical underpinning.

The fact that my training was integrative was significant for me as I believe that all the approaches I studied inform and influence each other.

This fits in with my personal philosophy of life. I believe that all sentient beings are strongly dominated by somatisation and awareness of the psychodynamic approach helps that energy to be shifted therapeutically and new energy can be released to enable the individual to become more in touch with themselves and more interconnected with others. Knowledge and awareness of our earliest stages of development provide the foundation for all later development and transformation. I believe that you must have a strong scaffolding before you can build on it, i.e., cultivate ego strength and identity which Ken Wilber calls, 'Centauric Awareness' (1996). Through this cultivation we acknowledge the significance of our phenomenological experiencing and our interrelationship with self and others.

Purist person-centred counsellor

Reasons for choosing the course

Prior to doing a Diploma in Person Centred Counselling I had studied and taught psychology for several years, so I felt that I had some familiarity with a range of approaches to counselling. I found all of them interesting, but there was something about the person-centred approach that resonated more strongly with me. I had also worked alongside some person-centred counsellors, so I feel that it had 'rubbed off' on me and by observing them I saw the importance of listening to others and being congruent. The non-directive nature of the approach had also made an impression on me: I had come to realise that the more I tried to help people and solve their problems, the more frustrated I became, and the greater people's expectations were of me. I gradually came to recognise the value in backing off rather than interfering and having more confidence in the capacity of others to figure things out for themselves. I didn't have to be the one with all the answers.

What the training involved

Even though I had read quite a lot about the person-centred approach, this had not prepared me for the experience of being on the course. It was student-led with minimal structure provided by the facilitators and whilst I was looking forward to the freedom that this promised, I had not anticipated just how disorienting and bewildering this could be. I hadn't realised how reliant I was on the norms of everyday life to tell me how to behave or who I was. Even things such as deciding when to break for lunch could involve lengthy discussion, or a tense silence during which everyone was waiting for someone else to say something. At times I was doubtful about aspects of my self-concept that I had previously taken for granted. In the course group I found myself behaving in ways that I struggled to accept or understand. Sometimes I would remain silent, fearful of talking too much and dominating the group, thereby silencing others. At other times I would feel free to speak if I wanted to, and then afterwards be left wondering why it had felt so important to say the things I said.

I also experienced strong feelings about other members of the course group – irritation, disdain, admiration, boredom. It was really difficult, especially at first, and there were moments when I could easily have stood up and walked out without returning. Instead, I learned to sit with those feelings rather than try to rid myself of them and it was a very humbling experience. I felt exposed a lot of the time, as if there was nowhere to hide and no reliable norms or social conventions to hide behind. I slowly learned to be seen by others as I truly was, and to let go of the larger-than-life persona I had spent many years constructing in order to conceal myself. I became more able to be present so that the group could accept me, and I could begin to accept myself.

Ponder points

Having read these accounts, what were the main reasons why the therapists chose their training pathways?

What will you bear in mind when choosing your type of training in line with these factors?

Conclusion

This chapter has examined the reasons why people choose their courses of study in counselling or choose to become a specific type of therapist. I have shared my experiences, and we have looked at the accounts of other practitioners. I hope you have become more aware of the different factors you need to consider when choosing your pathway to becoming a therapist.

As part of this we looked very briefly at several theoretical approaches and an exercise was offered to help you to become more aware of the modalities which are more suited to your beliefs and values. (See the answers at the end of this chapter.)

Choosing the right training for you may be one of the most important decisions you make so it needs to be done intentionally not lightly as this course gives you the foundation to be effective as a therapist and the grounding to work safely as a professional.

Quiz answers

If you have answered true to 1, 3, 7, 12, you are leaning more towards psychodynamic theory as these are some of the aspects underpinning this.

With 5, 6, 9, 14 you are taking more of a humanistic/person-centred view of human nature and helping.

Statements 10, 11, 13 and possibly 8 relate more to a behavioural or cognitive behavioural way of thinking and working.

If you said 'true' to 2, 8 and possibly 15 you may be of the view that one approach or theory is not enough to work with a range of issues and an integrative approach is needed to help people in distress. The model you choose to train in might be integrated by the focus on the therapeutic relationship.

Finally, it is true that some people cannot be helped by therapy of any kind (4) and yes, the therapeutic relationship is important in all types of counselling and therapy as I mentioned earlier (15).

If you have agreed with a wide range of these statements, it may be that you are really inclined towards training in an integrative way as you believe that a range of factors affect the way we are as people and the way we can be helped through therapy.

Notes

1 Systemic therapy focuses on the interactions and relationships between a group of people to help them address any problems and to move on.
2 This is a diagram tool to map a family and pattern of relationships (McGoldrick, Gerson and Petry, 2008).
3 Object relations – a theory developed by Melanie Klein to look at how 'human relationships are imagined and represented mentally by each individual' (Hough, 2021, p. 126).
4 Erikson is famous for his stages of psychosocial development across the lifespan rather than just the early life as with Freud (see Hough, 2021, pp. 122–124).

References

BACP (n.d.) What is systemic therapy? Available from www.bacp.co.uk/about-therapy/types-of-therapy/systemic-therapy [date accessed 2 October, 2024].

Cooper, M. (2008) The facts are friendly. *Therapy Today*, 19(7), 8–13.

Hough, M. (2021) *Counselling Skills and Theory*. London: Hodder Education.

McGoldrick, M., Gerson, R., and Petry, S. (2008) *Genograms: Assessment and Intervention*, 3rd edn. New York: Norton.

Norcross J. C. (2002) *Psychotherapy Relationships that Work: Therapist Contributions and Responsiveness to Patients*. New York: Oxford University Press.

Reeves, A. (2022) *An Introduction to Counselling and Psychotherapy*. London: Sage.

Sanders, P., Williams, P. J., and Rogers, A. (2021) *First Steps in Counselling: An Introductory Companion*. Monmouth: PCCS Books.

Short, F. and Thomas, P. (2015) *Core Approaches in Counselling and Psychotherapy*. London: Routledge.

Chapter 8

The importance of the experiential group

Tara Fox

Introduction

Learning together in a group can be meaningful and inspirational, offering you the chance to build bonds with other students and helping you to feel supported. The group experience offers considerable amounts of learning opportunities, often guided by the facilitator but also peer-led interactions for example a student might share something they have realised about themselves this week and the learning inspires the whole group.

This chapter will look at the importance of the group experience, including the personal development (PD) group and the course group. I will highlight the value of relational connection in becoming a counsellor drawing on my extensive experiences of personal development group facilitation, course leadership and research into this area. The pros and cons of the group experience will be presented so that you may prepare yourself a little for the experiential group and decide what you may need to confront about yourself compassionately. Overall, I hope you will understand more about how you can personally grow in a group through an active process of being present, thinking about your thinking, and sharing your insights with others.

In this chapter I will help you understand:

- how to prepare to meet the group
- my personal style of relating
- group process is 'a thing'
- how group facilitation will differ depending on the training course
- personal relationship difficulties
- the use of grounding interventions
- the pros and cons of the experiential group.

The etymology of the word experiential from the Latin 'experientia' meaning 'knowledge gained by testing or trials' (Online Etymology Dictionary, 2024) reminds us how through the group experience there is an opportunity for experimenting with new ways of relating to others. As each person puts their

DOI: 10.4324/9781003405757-9

foot in the water the hope is that the reaction will be supportive and if this is the case students can continue to grow in self-awareness and relational connection.

Preparing to meet the group

Preparing to meet your course may involve some imagination on your part as to what the group will be like. These thoughts may be in the background but when you enter the training environment, they are likely to influence how you feel. It is worth reflecting on what you are imagining bringing forward your self-awareness of the preconceptions and preoccupations you have.

Activity

- Who do you imagine will be there?
- What do you think the trainer will be like?
- How do you think people might see you?
- What will you want to show them?
- What will you want to hide?

Keeping an open mind frees you up to new possibilities whereas having fixed ideas about how things will play out on the course may limit your opportunity to see something new. You may find this hard and if this is the case be sure to register any differences to your imagined outcomes. Usually, at the start, educators will invite the group to say something about their hopes and fears for the course. If so, there is a space for you to express what the initial training group experience was like and if this was how you imagined it. In my experience, both as a student and a group facilitator, saying it out loud feels like a testing out and a personal challenge. And if others smile at you warmly and the tutor nods and accepts your opinion as valid then it starts a process of feeling safe in the group setting.

Is it safe in here?

Is it safe in here? This is likely to be your main concern upon entering the experiential group, process group, personal development (PD) group, encounter group or awareness group. All these words provide clues as to what happens in these spaces. You will have experiences in a group setting that can be utilised to develop your self-awareness and personal growth especially if you reflect upon these experiences openly in the group and 'process' them. To get the best out of the group you will need to share something of yourself. If you do not share nobody knows what you are thinking and feeling. Others may assume to know (fill in the gaps) and whatever they imagine can influence how they are around you, leading to it being challenging in the group.

You may have decided at some point in your life that being quiet means you don't have to get involved in other people's business but unfortunately this is unlikely to serve you well in this situation.

Personal style of relating quiz

- How are you at talking in a group?
- How do you feel sharing your thoughts?
- How do you feel sharing your feelings?
- How do you feel about disagreeing with other people's views?
- What have your previous experiences of groupwork been like?
- Do you worry about taking up too much time in a group?
- Would you feel OK being upset or crying in a group?
- Are you often worried about being judged?

Having answered these questions, see the personal experience of a student below.

Case study: Josie

I had many problems at school with people poking their noses into each other's business. There was so much drama with arguments on social media and I felt like I wanted to be invisible. I decided after I left school that it was easier to keep out of people's problems and if I was quiet no one would pick fault with me. In the counselling training group, I realised people actually wanted to hear from me and I had to push myself to say something. The more I was quiet the more anxious I felt. One day I burst into tears and explained how the silent moments made me feel under pressure and I was sorry for not being able to speak up, but this was so hard for me. The group was really moved by my reaction and a few people spoke up saying they had been worrying about me wondering if I was Ok. Someone said they were so relieved to know that I did not dislike them as they imagined I was looking down my nose at them. Other people shared their worries too and the whole group felt different after that day. We seemed to bond more, and it started to feel safer in there.

Does any of this resonate with you? I have experienced this many times in the experiential group and from the facilitator's perspective this encounter shows a lot of courage, humility, and wisdom to reach out. These characteristics are stated in the BACP ethical framework for good practice in the professions (2018). It is a sign of strength to be vulnerable and take a risk to experiment with new ways of relating to others. It helps everyone else shift up a gear to dare to be more authentic and releases energy trapped by fears in the group.

Rogers spoke about the need for psychological contact as the first step for therapeutic work to occur (Rogers, 1957). Equally being available for contact with your peers will help you all to develop trust in the group process.

Group process: A process is a thing!

Rogers once said, 'in the group we are wiser than we know' (Rogers, 1970) which I find inspirational and in alignment with my experiences. I have reflected on this to mean our untapped knowledge; our unknown potential is larger than what we may anticipate. In the group, we have the potential to expand our awareness and elevate our growth. Try to trust the process of being with each other even when you don't know where you are going you are still not where you were at the start. Facilitators should attend to the group process periodically to restore awareness of the boundaries of the space and your role within it. There is no fast track through the experiential group encounter, and I find the children's story book *We're Going on a Bear Hunt* by Michael Rosen and Helen Oxenbury helpful:

> We can't go over it, we can't go under it, oh no we'll have to go through it.

I recall spending many weeks sitting with a group that had been given clear explanations as to the purpose of the PD group. The learning outcomes and aim of the group had been presented and read by all of the members, but still something was getting in the way for several students. While some had got used to the idea that they may be sitting with uncertainty and that was part of the process others were still questioning why and what the purpose is.

One student expressed resentment – 'I did not sign up for this!' Eventually, those members realised that they were 'doing PD' because they were in a process which is a thing in itself! Mezirow's ten phases of transformational learning begin with a 'disorientating dilemma' of which the PD group is and ends with a 'reintegration of a new perspective' (Mezirow, 1981, p. 65) and I think this sums up the group process succinctly. However, feeling disorientated is tricky to deal with. Students frequently describe this emotion as 'discombobulated' and sharing your sense of discombobulation helps everyone to recognise this within themselves, engage in self-reflection, and share new insights. Of course, there is much joy to share too as their confidence increases through feedback, client work, and appreciation of their unique offering to the profession.

The facilitator: Different approaches

Whatever training route you have chosen should be modelled by the facilitator. For example, if you are on a person-centred psychotherapy training programme then your group facilitator should embody those characteristics, and each member aims to offer empathy, unconditional positive regard and congruence (core conditions). Here are some examples of how facilitators from different approaches might conduct a group.

A Gestalt leader will see the group as a social system where people relate in degrees of separateness and unity. The leader will help members to notice how they block, invite contact and will share their own internal process of what they feel, witness and ideas about what may be happening. They will draw from knowledge of group dynamics for example the norms that seem to be present in the group like 'it is not ok to disagree with each other' or 'person x seems to be the one who knows the answers.' Three levels are occurring for the leader – the interpersonal growth of each member, the intrapersonal connection (between others) and the overall growth of the group as a social system. They may use Gestalt methods and techniques to teach phenomenological processes.

Transactional Analysis leaders of process groups will similarly help members to be aware of relational styles and intrapsychic dynamics (stoke economy, transactions, games, drivers). Within this process the leader will have an eye on transference and countertransference and will use transactional analysis theory to activate the adult, analyse psychological games and enhance new decisions.

Integrative relational approaches

The space between each of us in the room is sometimes called the 'inter-subjective space' and this is where you connect to others and others connect to you. Subjective experiences of another person's life are understood through your relationship with the other. Relational approaches recognise it is the vehicle of the relationship that heals the client, the co-created collaboration of client and therapists who respond to each other in the here and now.

The facilitator will respond to the 'here and now' (what is happening in the moment) to work with one member of the group as well as attending to the group space. Facilitators will likely share their 'felt sense' or what they feel about the group energy and invite members to share their experience of this. Due to the embodied nature of interactions, this approach is highly challenging and requires trust in the process.

O'Hara (2003) stresses how it is important that the facilitator lets go of being an expert and risks feeling vulnerable to engage in learning through the process thus acting as a good role model for others. This can be challenging as students will naturally look to the facilitator for expert guidance on personal development matters. For more about the facilitator's experiences, my co-author Jayne has written a chapter about the role if you want to know more (Godward, 2020).

My style of facilitation is inspired by Rogers' encounter groups, Yalom's existential approach to groups and Neff's self-compassion (2003) particularly that we all suffer and sharing our suffering normalises any fears and creates a sense of shared humanity, a common ground where we feel a connection with others in the here and now.

I recall that in the early days of PD group facilitation, I was caught up in getting the role right to the cost of appreciating my autonomy. It was not what I should do in the moment but what I chose to do in the moment that mattered. Recognising this took the pressure off and helped me to work more authentically in the moment as I would do with clients. This echoes how students feel too at the start initially thinking there are rules for being an ideal counsellor rather than their genuine use of self. Being genuine and able to relate in a group may be a challenge especially when you have past difficulties.

Personal relationship difficulties

Previous adverse childhood experiences may affect the enjoyability of the experiential group in some circumstances. Life events such as parental divorce and bereavement, abuse issues like bullying and assault can resurface if mentioned by others and re-experienced through misunderstandings or conflicts in the group. Being part of an experiential group requires the use of the reflective function, the capacity to mentalise, meaning the ability to think about states of mind including thoughts, feelings, and intentions in the self and others. Equally, you need to have what is known as a meta-perspective where you can notice your reactions, feelings, and thoughts and decide upon what you will do next (thinking about thinking). This is required when working with clients too, so the group experience helps you to practice the use of your reflective function. For more about this see the work of Peter Fonagy who has written and researched a great deal on this topic including the creation of a Reflective Function Scale. (Fonagy et al., 1991; 2016). Mindfulness based interventions (MBI) have been known to impact positively on our ability to notice what we are noticing and to take a step back to choose how to react and what to say.

Interventions to keep grounded

Being affected by other people's experiences and feelings can be the downside to being part of the course group but the work itself brings us into contact with all aspects of human life from suffering to joyfulness therefore part of the preparation for client work lies in the group experience. In Chapter 13 'Self care: Boundaries, not bubble bath!' I have focused on helpful strategies for therapist self-care but here I wish to mention how you can foster a sense of grounding in the group with others.

Charura (2020) reminds us to acknowledge differences as a key part of the process where group members 'stand counter' to each other. In my experience, students seek to be similar to others in order to connect, however, it is only through the respectful appreciation of differences in experiences that space for connection and growth is created. Students realise 'yes, we have both had that issue, but we have experienced it uniquely.'

It is better to work on separating your own perspective from other people's stories. This is where grounding and mindful awareness can help. This requires you to be here and not somewhere else. See the following example where Jo struggles to be here in the room.

Case study: Jo

What's for tea?

I do not want to be here. I need to think about what's for tea and plan the shopping list in my head. Then I won't be troubled by what's going on in here today. I just want to get it over and done with so I can get on with the real reason I am here which is to learn something.

How can this help and hinder Jo if they continue in this way? How might this impact on the group?

Being here is important for the work you will do with clients. Colismo and Pos (2015) have written a lot about the need for therapist presence and how this can help the client. Therapeutic Presence involves the therapist being fully in the moment with the client with the intent or purpose of being of service to a healing process (Colismo and Pos, 2015).

The following two exercises adapted from Geller, Pos and Colismo (2012) helps to ground you in your own body, maintaining the boundary between you and others. I recommend you practice the following before entering the group:

Grounding exercise to prepare you for the group

Keep your feet about a foot distance apart from each other and lower your gaze to keep a focus on your feet.

Notice the left foot and gain a sense of this foot touching the ground.

Notice the right foot and sense of this foot making contact with the ground.

Breathe into the centre of your body.

Gently move your weight from one foot to the other to feel a balance and energy in your feet.

Imagine a silver thread pulling the top of your head above you.

Return your awareness to your feet once more and breathe into the centre of your body.

Grounding in the group:

In the group itself bring your awareness to the feeling of your feet as you sit in the group whenever you need to. Bring your focus to the feeling of your bottom in the seat or your back as it rests in the chair. As you listen to other people try to visualise the opening of a basket of material in front of each group member. After they have finished speaking imagine the basket lid is folding closed again, packed away once more.

Again, these techniques can help you to be grounded when in groups. This can help those of you who are highly empathic to see those problems belong to the other person, and they have the power to close it down when they wish and take it away with them.

The pros and cons of the experiential group

Although everyone experiences the experiential group uniquely there are themes that crop up for students year on year. I have summarised these in the table below:

Pros	Cons
Creates emotional learning	Emotionally impacts on you
Facilitates knowledge of our responses to others	Group interactions can bring up memories from the past
Experiences are impactful	Needs time to reflect upon and make meaning
Contributes significant material for your journal reflections	Requires you to make a deliberate conscious effort to learn from experiences
Provides the opportunity to make sense of experiences together	The uncertainty can be challenging
Gives you the chance to practice sitting with others' emotions without trying to fix it	Anxiety provoking
Good role modelling from the facilitator	Poor facilitation can retraumatise students when support is needed and not offered
Provides an open space to feel the core conditions	Requires psychological contact
A chance to encounter difference and acceptance of this	Increases awareness of prejudices and oppression

Carole Smith from the University of Huddersfield conducted qualitative research with qualified counsellors and psychotherapists exploring the PD group experience for her PhD. Her research findings show positive themes of increased self-awareness, making use of PD experiences in client work and learning emotional depth. Challenging themes were found to be emotional disruption, the impact of past life experiences, learning tolerance to stay with emotions, and the requirement of reflection skills (Smith, 2020, pp. 54–59).

There is much to process from the group experience and a lot to work through. I acknowledge how painful this can be for some students and the findings from Carole's research add more evidence to the literature on how important the facilitator role is in creating safety for members. Robson and Robson (2008) found that some students felt traumatised and their study questioned the safety of the group as a learning tool if the facilitator lacks the ability to respond and intervene to address emotional disruption between members.

Conclusion

This chapter has looked at the importance of the group experience in your journey towards becoming a therapist. It helps to prepare you a little for the experiential group and to decide what you may need to be aware of.

Overall, I hope you can see the power of the group experience in helping you to grow personally and professionally through an active process of engaging, sharing and supporting. The pros and cons of the experience can help you to identify anything that you may find challenging, and my hope is you can reach out for help when needed. Equally, you will see how the group experience can be transformative developing you beyond what may be possible when learning alone. Practising grounding activities will go a long way to keeping you robust through the group process and to giving you a safer experience of the uncertainty of the group encounter.

References

Colismo, K. and Pos, A. (2015) A rational model of expressed therapeutic presence. *Journal of Psychotherapy Integration*, 25(2), 0–114.

Charura, D. (2020) Psychotherapists' experiences of co-facilitating large encounter PCEP groups: An interpretative phenomenological analysis of six interviews. *Person-Centered & Experiential Psychotherapies*, 19(3), 251–270.

Fonagy, P., Steele, M., Steele, H., Moran, G. S., and Higgitt, A. C. (1991) The capacity for understanding mental states: The reflective self in parent and child and its significance for security of attachment. *Infant Mental Health Journal*, 12(3), 201–218.

Fonagy, P., Luyten, P., Moulton-Perkins, A., Lee, Y.-W., Warren, F., Howard, S., Ghinai, R., Fearon, P., and Lowyck, B. (2016) Development and validation of a self-report measure of mentalizing: The reflective functioning questionnaire, *PLOS ONE*, 11(7).

Geller, S.M., Pos, A., and Colismo, K. (2012) Therapeutic presence: A fundamental common factor in the provision of effective psychotherapy. *Society for Psychotherapy Integration*, 47(3), 6–13.

Godward, J. (2020) Experiences of running personal development groups: The facilitator role. In Godward, J., Dale, H., and Smith, C. (Eds), *Personal Development Groups for Trainee Counsellors: An Essential Companion*. Oxford: Routledge.

Mezirow, J. (1981) *A Critical Theory of Adult Learning and Education. Experience and Learning: Reflection at Work. Adults Learning in the Workplace: Part A*. Victoria, Australia. Deakin University.

Neff, K. D. (2003). Self-compassion: An alternative conceptualization of a healthy attitude toward oneself. *Self and Identity*, 2(2), 85–101.

Online Etymology Dictionary (2024). Experiential (adj.). Available from www.etym online.com/search?q=experiential [date accessed 18 November, 2023].

O'Hara, M. (2003). Cultivating consciousness: Carl R. Rogers's person-centered group process as transformative androgogy. *Journal of Transformative Education*, 1(1), 64–79.

Rogers, C. R. (1957). The necessary and sufficient conditions of therapeutic personality change. *Journal of Consulting Psychology*, 21(2), 95–103.

Rogers, C. R. (1970) *On Encounter Groups*. New York: Harper Books.

Rosen, M. and Oxenbury, H. (2016) *We're Going on a Bear Hunt*. London: Walker Books Ltd.

Smith, C. (2020) Experiences of personal development groups: A research base. In Godward, J., Dale, H., and Smith, C. (Eds), *Personal Development Groups for Trainee Counsellors: An Essential Companion* (pp. 54–59). Oxford: Routledge.

Chapter 9

The shift

Becoming a counsellor

Jayne Godward

Introduction

The whole of this book is concerned with the process and steps to becoming a counsellor. This chapter addresses the nub of the issue as to what are the personal changes which need to occur so that students can develop into counsellors who are resilient and competent to do therapeutic work.

Tara and I named this 'the shift' – a movement or transformation in the self which is important particularly for working relationally with others.

This chapter is an exploration of what this shift means bearing in mind that it can mean different things to different trainees as we are all unique and make sense of our experiences in our own ways.

We begin by looking at the tutor viewpoint then move on to look at some accounts by recently qualified counsellors.

So, the chapter will include:

- tutor views on the shift
- accounts from recent trainees
- some discussion of these accounts.

Ponder points

What do you think needs to happen for people to develop into counsellors?
What personal changes need to occur for them to become effective and able to cope with the demands of the work?

The tutor viewpoint

Jayne's perspective

From a personal point of view based on my own experience and what I have observed as a counsellor trainer since 2006, becoming more self-aware and

DOI: 10.4324/9781003405757-10

understanding yourself and your history is a big part of personal develop-ment. The training encourages students to look at difficult parts of themselves and their lives and they look at how past life events have shaped them. Students start to realise the impact of their personal history and how they have made sense of the world. A key thing for me as for many students was to become more accepting of myself which led to more acceptance of others too.

As people become more self-aware and develop, they start to decide what is ok and what isn't in terms of relationships with others and what kind of person do they want to be. Some of this might be linked to our conditions of worth which were the expectations from our significant others including how we think we should behave, think and feel. (Short and Thomas, 2015, p. 97)

Many trainees say they are people pleasers or find it hard to put themselves and their needs before others. Some of this may be linked to their upbringing or culture. Part of training involves dissolving these conditions of worth and becoming more confident in our own judgements rather than looking to others for approval. This can feel like a freeing process and may feel like a weight has been lifted. As the practitioner course progresses, I have noticed students start to set more personal boundaries and are less likely to be manipulated by others. They may take care of themselves and know their limits more. With increased self-respect and confidence, students tend to become more assertive in their relationships and are less willing to do things they don't agree with just to fit in or to please.

Case study: Maarya

Maarya had been brought up to always put her elders first and to look after others before herself (her conditions of worth). During her younger life this was sustainable but later when she had her own family and increasingly poor health, this became diffi-cult, as she was exhausted and was starting to suffer from depression. She would feel guilty if she could not respond promptly to the needs of her husband's parents as it was part of her duty as a good daughter-in-law. As she progressed with her counsellor training, she realised that she couldn't do everything and started to see her role as a 'people- pleaser' and realised that she had lost a sense of who she was as a person. Gradually she started to put in boundaries and seek help from others in her family so that she could manage conflicting loyalties and responsibilities. She realised later that if she hadn't have done this, she would have been seriously ill and would not have been able to look after anyone or complete her training in which she had invested a lot.

Tara's perspective

I have noticed that students feel a shift when they reconcile their past with their new identity as counsellor. This involves coming to terms with and accepting what has gone before and gaining a new perspective on their capabilities. A sort of realisation that they have the power and agency to change and be the best person they want to be. An inner trust in their internal wisdom and intuition grows bringing an awareness of safety in their own bodies to trust themselves, be with uncertainty, and trust the process of therapy. This is also my own story.

Sometimes the course helps you to have a reflective space to make sense of adverse experiences which have shaped your personal development rather than the shift taking place on the course itself.

So, what has this got to do with being an effective counsellor?

Being more congruent in yourself or authentic to yourself and feeling more grounded will help you to help others and the former is one of six necessary and sufficient conditions identified by Carl Rogers (1957) for working therapeutically.

What is useful here is that as a student you will probably go through a similar process to some of your clients, so this will help you to understand what this involves and how difficult but enlightening this can be. See Tolan (2012) for an explanation of the seven stages of process first identified by Rogers (1961) describing personality change.

Becoming more self-aware helps us recognise our motives and helps us be more aware of our personal difficulties and triggers which could interfere with the client work. We explored this in Chapter 2 on motivations.

Increased confidence but being aware of our limitations may help us become more genuine with others and more humble, having more compassion for the struggles of our clients. It may help us get 'alongside' them and increase our empathy of their difficulties.

As I said before, being more self-accepting generally helps us accept others and means we are not putting up barriers to protect ourselves. This openness and possibly approachability is a big bonus in client work.

Mearns and Thorne (2011, p. 45) talk about the importance of the counsellor's attitude to themselves and how self-acceptance is essential for work with clients. They go so far to say that 'it is impossible to offer a client acceptance, empathy and genuineness at the deepest level if such responses are withheld from the self.'

Views of recent trainees

Three qualified counsellors who are recently trained from different walks of life and different courses answered questions about the shift. In this section we read their accounts. The questions posed were:

- What were the major shifts and changes you experienced which were essential to you to be able to do therapeutic work?
- How did this experience of change feel overall?

Each of them chose a pseudonym and wrote a little introduction to themselves.

Ponder points

Whilst reading about these experiences think about the following:

- Are there any common themes in the accounts regarding the process these counsellors went through?
- What are the key aspects which made up the shift for these individuals?

Experience 1: Yvette

I am Yvette, a North American transplant in the UK who recently embarked on a midlife career change after a period of existential contemplation following experiences around illness and bereavement. I am a mother, friend, music lover and active citizen.

> When trying to describe my experience of training to be a counsellor to others, I often say it felt like being turned inside out and back again, a process which has been both painful and empowering in equal measure. I began my journey to become a counsellor with the notion I understood who I was, viewing myself as independent, resilient, kind and a bit of a people-pleaser. I also begrudgingly admitted a tendency towards impatience and reactivity. I found I could easily form relationships and considered my attachment style to be secure.
>
> But as I delved deeper into my studies around relationships and attachment, I was prompted to more closely examine how I interacted with others, uncovering my avoidant tendencies in certain situations. I explored the likely roots of this avoidance – my relationship with a chronically anxious and sometimes volatile mother – and subsequent triggers – when I feel vulnerable, or when I fear that my shadow side may be exposed.
>
> Confronting these aspects of myself has allowed me to understand the cost to my personal relationships, but also how it had the potential to impact my therapeutic work. To mitigate this, I worked with my supervisor, pinpointing scenarios which might trigger my avoidance. I also used personal therapy and my Personal and Professional Development (PPD) sessions to practice being more open and honest about this side of me.
>
> This process has given me insight into the experience of my clients, and how difficult it is to be completely open with oneself or another. It has reinforced the centrality of the therapeutic relationship in creating a path to change or healing and has made me reflect upon how I might use my own experience to model insight and growth. Whilst I may not explicitly

share what I have experienced, I feel there are ways that this can be communicated without words, but rather through human connection.

My training has also involved exploration of my identity as an 'outsider.' Born and raised outside of the UK, I have felt mostly welcome into and a part of the community I call home. I have always been aware of my difference, but have seen it as an advantage, serving as an easy icebreaker in new social situations and boosting my confidence in such encounters. But over time, the differences have taken on new meaning. Many in my community have never 'left home' and live near family and childhood friends, which can leave me feeling isolated from shared histories, prompting an unconscious withdrawal.

Confronting this in therapy has been a painful process, but addressing the sorrow and loss beneath has helped me come to terms with complicated feelings. It has also helped me to realise that when I disengage from those around me, it can exacerbate my sense of being out of place or untethered. I understand how I might be perceived by others as judgemental or cold in such moments, which will be confusing when I am typically warm and open. Awareness has helped me recognise when these feelings emerge, allowing me to my defensive or avoidant reactions. This is especially important in my work with clients.

Discussing my 'outsider' status in PPD has also been important. I typically feel embarrassed to complain from my privileged place in the migrant pecking order, but members of the group generously provided me space without judgement. And though I do not carry the trauma of war, persecution, racism or xenophobia experienced by others who have left their home countries, I have some insight into how culture and place can impact identity, and how I can approach this with sensitivity and curiosity in the therapeutic space.

PPD also allowed me to explore how I deal with conflict, observing how I oscillate between problem solving or trying to soothe conflict to impatience and a struggle to find empathy. Paying closer attention to my initial reactions to others has allowed me to explore what might be playing out for me, and how I might respond in ways that are both honest and empathic. This is not always the easiest path for the people-pleaser in me, but it has also given me greater skills to reflect and repair, which is crucial for my work as a counsellor.

I am filled with gratitude for this experience, which has not only prepared me for work as a therapist, but also made me more engaged and aware of my impact on others, especially as mother, partner, daughter, sibling and friend.

Comment: This person has really made use of her personal therapy, personal and professional development groupwork and supervision to gain more understanding of her identity and patterns of relating. It is really clear here how the process of change and attending therapy has informed her work with clients and has helped her to understand the process they will go through. The impact of the shift is not just enabling her to work effectively with clients but also relate better to others in her personal relationships.

Experience 2: Keir

I am a person-centred private practice counsellor based in Yorkshire. I work in disability advocacy services. Fairness, being kind to others and justice are part of who I am. My identity is grounded in treating people with dignity and respect. I love being around others and offering people time and space to be themselves.

> Looking back over my counselling training, one of the key moments for me was my newfound ability to express myself in front of others within the group without my own trauma overwhelming me. It was the moment where I could confidently share that I had been subject to abuse and say it without experiencing a complete emotional breakdown. I had worked through personal therapy and reached a place where I felt I had received the conditions from the group that enabled me to take down my emotional barriers. This was a liberating experience and in tandem with having my first client at my placement, it created a sense of confidence in me. I realised that I was meant to be on the course, as the feedback I was getting from clients was cementing a new identity in me as a counsellor who could help people effectively and was making a genuine difference in their lives.
>
> Another point where I felt the shift in my experience was about three quarters of the way through my 100 hours placement, as I began to reflect on those initial first sessions, realising just how many people I had supported in that period. I comprehended the differences in my confidence from client one to the point I had reached. Not only was I recognising this shift in myself, but I was also noticing my classmates as they were expressing themselves in the shoes of qualified counsellors, even though we were not yet finished the course. To me, this was the power of placement practice. Being a trainee practitioner at such an early stage offers students the opportunity to own their role before they officially have it, granting them great responsibility so early in the training. The combination of emotionally moving on from guarding hidden parts of myself and the realisation of what I had achieved in my placement hours were pivotal moments of shift for me as I grew into the role of a competent counsellor.
>
> The shift led me to make changes not only in my professional life but also in my personal life. I realised the depth of positive emotional health that comes from embracing change in general. I began to trust myself

more in my decisions, choosing to distance myself from people in my life who were emotionally holding me back. The most unusual feeling overall was the illumination of the negative parts of my life that the shift had revealed, it was like a light had been put on the things, people, and experiences that no longer served me. As I built emotional confidence in all areas of my life, I no longer felt worried about sharing my thoughts and feelings. I realised, through the group, that we were all fallible, we had all shown our insecurities and put ourselves out there emotionally.

It felt like a switch had flicked. When you spend four years of your life learning about yourself, your peers, and your clients week in and week out, the change happens naturally. I can only describe it as a beautiful experience. Although I know it is a common experience, it felt so special at the same time.

Comment: This account emphasises what the shift involves in terms of developing the counsellor identity. After developing more openness with others as a result of his personal therapy, this person started to develop confidence and to feel more like a counsellor taking on the professional role and the responsibility which goes with that. There is a real recognition of achievement here. A key part of the shift seems to have been about trusting oneself and understanding negative aspects of one's life then moving on. Recognising that it is ok to be vulnerable and emotional played a big part. Here again the shift impacted on both professional and personal relationships. There is a real recognition of how special the personal learning experience has been.

Gemma

I am a counsellor working with children, young people and adults.

The person I was before completing my counselling training would not have been capable of the therapeutic work that I have done since and continue to do now. The comfort that I have found in understanding myself on a much deeper level has brought about a quiet confidence in my work that would not have been achievable before.

Being able to understand myself and piece together things that had happened in my life and how they had affected me brought a lot of inner peace. It felt like each week I was finding parts to my jigsaw that had never been seen before and this understanding brought about an acceptance in who I am, who I had been and where I had been let down. It enabled me to forgive myself for feeling so different and out of place for most of my life.

On a practical level I would never have had the confidence to apply for a job, attend an interview and believe I could actually be successful. On an emotional level I wouldn't have had the capacity to hear a client's story, sit with them through their exploration of their difficulties and witness their journey. My level of anxiety, worry, fear and panic would have sat in the way of any therapeutic work and I would not have been able to meet the client at that deeper level.

To most people it would not be obvious the changes that took place in myself during my counsellor training, but to me it feels like I am almost a different person. It feels like all the worry and anxiety that I was carrying around over the simplest things has drifted away and every day is much easier. I recently walked into a coffee shop to grab a drink and snack, and it hit me that a few years previously the build up to doing that would have been incredibly heavy, to the point where I may not have even bothered. I would have been worrying what people in the queue were thinking about me, worrying about what to say (and rehearsing it over and over), worrying I would say something stupid and panicking I would pick up someone else's drink or they would pick up mine and what would happen then. That is just one small example of what my day would look like without adding in anything particularly difficult or different. I still do feel anxious or worried at times but usually about something much bigger like an interview or meeting a new client for the first time. Everything is so much more manageable and the freedom I feel from releasing these almost crippling feelings is life changing in a very quiet way.

Interesting I also find it a lot easier to set and hold boundaries with people in my life and have honest and open conversations rather than avoiding any chance of perceived confrontation. This has enabled me to have stronger relationships with the people who are important to me and let go of those who aren't.

Comment: Here the shift involved a deeper understanding of self and a real increase in self-confidence. Here again there is evidence of self-acceptance. This person went through a process of overcoming anxiety and worry which enabled her to form relationships with clients. The sense is of someone who became more grounded and ok within herself enabling her to feel ok with others. There is a sense of freeing up and of being lighter. Relating to others has become easier and has strengthened some relationships whilst others have been let go.

Ponder points

Were you surprised to read the processes these therapists went through? Or were you expecting some of this?
How have these changes enabled them to work with clients?
What changes in yourself are you anticipating as you embark on your counsellor/ therapy training?

Conclusion

This chapter aimed to explain what we had termed 'the shift' which was usually a series of personal changes and transformations that take place within a trainee as they progress on their counsellor or therapist training. Tara and I shared our views on this from what we have observed whilst training students and thanks to the honest accounts of fairly recent trainees, we read what this involved and the life changing aspects from first-hand experience. This 'shift' not only affected the person's self-concept and sense of identity but also their ability to manage both professional and personal relationships.

References

Mearns, D. and Thorne, B. (2011) *Person-Centred Counselling in Action*. London: Sage.

Rogers, C. R. (1957) The necessary and sufficient condition of therapeutic personality change. *Journal of Consulting Psychology*, 21, 95–103.

Rogers, C. R. (1961) *On Becoming a Person*. London: Constable.

Short, F. and Thomas, P. (2015) *Core Approaches in Counselling and Psychotherapy*. London: Routledge.

Tolan, J. (2012) *Skills in Person-Centred Counselling*. London: Sage.

Chapter 10

Barriers to development

Tara Fox

Introduction

This chapter considers how your reactions to the course expectations and demands of training can be a barrier to development. These include your responses to the academic requirements, your resilience and your willingness to develop from receiving feedback and learn from your mistakes. Your professional training course requires ongoing learning from experiences of client work by reflecting on the self. This endeavour is a humbling experience that might involve self-doubt and worry but also creates opportunities for self-exploration and discovery about your ability to be therapeutic.

Equally past educational experiences and previous relationships with educators and those in positions of power can affect student development including unresolved relational difficulties. This can position trainees as vulnerable learners struggling to strive in a high-intensity personal development environment.

This chapter wishes to normalise typical barriers to development and reframe these as opportunities to grow in the face of adversity. It aims to help you reflect upon and confront your reactions to training expectations and consider ways to address these.

It will look at:

- humility in training
- resilient qualities for learning
- fitness to practice
- responding to feedback from others
- reframing problems to opportunities
- is this the right time?
- typical barriers experienced by trainees
- Kahler's Drivers (1975) as one way of understanding how we can react to expectations
- recognising your own drivers
- the success iceberg.

DOI: 10.4324/9781003405757-11

The need for humility in training

In my experience, many students who decide to train as a therapist have already had a successful professional life and the decision to train as a psychotherapist is a secondary career. It can feel daunting being at the beginning again and self-esteem can be fragile. Our job roles form a big part of our identity often gifting us self-confidence born out of our success. Being so successful in these careers can make it harder to develop the humility needed for self-awareness and self-growth (Akhtar, 2018).

Becoming humbled is one of the things students talk about a lot during their professional counselling training and client work. Humility is a quality 'a self-view that something greater than the self exists' (Ou et al., 2014, p. 37). It occurs through a process whereby you allow yourself to be teachable. I recall a humorous moment in a teaching session where I invited a group of professionals to complete a SWOT (Strengths, Weaknesses, Opportunities and Threats) analysis. This involved consideration of one's strengths and weaknesses, opportunities for growth and any threats to achieving these. A student who was also a solicitor was struggling with the exercise and explained he had no weaknesses. His co-practice manager, also a solicitor gave me a wink as she knew this was not the case, but he was finding it hard to confront and refused to do the SWOT. He decided the course was not for him and here we can see how hard it can be to have a degree of humility to open oneself up to self-discovery and development.

Equally, first-time career students bring so much wisdom from their life experiences yet often being younger than others may experience self-doubt and question their competence even though they may have good academic skills. Again, these worries can be a barrier to development.

What seemed like a good idea at the time of signing up can suddenly feel overwhelming when the course requirement elements become clearer and the reality of time constraints for wider placement responsibilities and academic assignments impact. Academic anxieties can greatly affect the enjoyment of counselling training. As people compare their assignment scores there can be a sense of failure, self-doubt about their ability to achieve, or conversely a sense of superiority and one-upmanship.

Increasing your resilience skills can support your growth when facing ongoing challenges and can be learned in tandem with the course. This can be embedded in the course structure as a way of fostering resilience such as practice opportunities, peer and self-evaluation, stepped approaches to scaffold you along the way, and an overall environment of safety where questions can be asked without feeling stupid. It can also be developed through deliberate training in resilience skills.

Resilient qualities

Being resilient is not about bouncing back from adversity per se but about the capacity to embrace the challenge and address the steps needed to learn and develop. According to Richardson's (2002, p. 207) definition, resilience is viewed as 'personal and interpersonal gifts and strengths that can be accessed to grow through adversity.' Personal disruption and adversity are viewed as presenting valuable opportunities for avenues of growth (Richardson, 1990).

Choosing to undertake professional training is a desire to have a planned disruption in your life to grow and develop into a professional counsellor or psychotherapist. Our capacity to grow through adversity involves embracing the experience and accepting the challenges so we can make a deliberate plan to face what is needed or expected from us in that moment. The Latin roots of the word capacity 'capere' (to take or hold) draw our attention to this willingness to embrace rather than resist the experience (Online Etymology Dictionary, 2024).

Take a look at the key characteristics of resilient people below adapted from Reivich and Shatte (2002). How able are you to do the following?

Resilient quality	Able to do? Yes/No
Stay flexible and open-minded – embracing difficulties and learning from them.	
Practice patience and kindness – self and others.	
Be flexible in your thinking and be optimistic.	
Being in the present moment -mindfulness; focus on what you can do in the present.	
Value and have good relationships – build your support system.	
Know and consider your limits including self-care practices.	
Know how to respond to feedback.	
Reflect on your experiences on your own and with others.	

Ponder points

- What change could you make now to help you?
- Who could assist you with this?
- How would you know things had improved?

I took a group of 72 counselling and mental health degree students through a 12-week resilience programme during their first year at university as a way of supporting their transition into the new learning environment and with the hope of building supportive relationships and mutuality in their onward journey through the course. The programme covered training in mindful awareness known to build distance between thoughts and reactions to more of an observer stance. Aspects of mindfulness-based cognitive therapy (Segal, Williams and Teasdale, 2002) were also covered to help students to reframe their unhelpful thoughts. Psychoeducation from neuroscience and applied positive psychology such as the science of gratitude (Hanson, 2014) were also covered.

I recommend you work on these in personal therapy and self-directed study. You could for example keep a diary of things you have appreciated each day. This could help you to retrain your brain to notice more of the good stuff that happens instead of just the difficult things. Our brains have a negativity bias to help us to be alert to danger so we need to work on our attention to positives. Ruby Wax has co-written a helpful book with a Monk and a Neuroscientist to help people understand how their mind works and how mindfulness can help (Wax, Ranpura, and Thubten, 2018). This is a good read and one I recommend.

During a focus group with seven participants discussing their experience of the resilience programme student data showed that compassionate facilitation of resilience training was beneficial for helping them to cope with the emotional and cognitive challenges of their educational experience but also life in general. This early intervention of resilience training during their first year helped students experience the new environment as safer and supportive, normalising student fears and instigating peer-supportive relationships. This was because hearing peers disclose similar fears and worries seemed to build trusting bonds, social connections, and a feeling of empowerment. Similarly, if you can share your feelings and any worries during training you are confronting your barriers to development and contributing to developing safer spaces for yourself and others. This takes courage and might feel risky but brave spaces seem to build more psychological safety when facilitated in a climate of compassion.

Fitness to practice issues

Fitness to practice issues could cause students to worry about reaching out to educators and student support services for mental health support during training. The Shadow Self (Jung, 1961) is usually kept hidden from others but during counselling training, there is an emphasis on self-reflection, especially in supervision, PD groups, and focused reflective assignments which may bring hidden traumas to the surface especially as psychotherapists are known to have higher rates of childhood trauma (Elliott and Guy, 1993). This can become a risk factor for working on placement with clients and is a potential barrier to the trainee's successful completion of their training. In a study by Cleary and Armour (2022) 'lived experience' counsellors/psychotherapists were found to struggle with integrating their patient and therapist identities, shifting between identifying as a therapist or patient depending on circumstances and therefore potentially impacting on client work through the countertransference (the therapists' emotional reaction to the client's story). The participants in this study felt that theoretical knowledge and personal therapy throughout training assisted in healing and recovery.

Equally working through one's own childhood history during training gives a special lens to empathise with clients yet can also be overwhelming when feelings are stirred up from the past and relived in the present in the counselling room or learning environment. A supportive course group serves as a secure base for a sense of belonging. Some students remain connected all of their lives to significant peers met through their training. Such bonds are reminders of who was there, who saw it, who remembers and who cared. I am still in touch with a woman I met during my initial training, and we love to know we went through it together, we saw what happened and we emotionally supported each other with our vulnerabilities.

Chapter 2 on motivations discusses the concept of the wounded healer where you can reflect on the value of being wounded, the gifts of these experiences for the work and the hindering aspects arising from past suffering. I have reflected on the Japanese art of golden joinery known as 'Kintsugi' where broken pottery is mended with gold and lacquer rather than masking the join with glue. A strong reminder that our flaws don't have to be concealed but celebrated making us stand out, shine and be stronger than before.

This process of embracing your vulnerabilities rather than using your energy to avoid them can be really uncomfortable but equally this is a natural part of training leading to the discovery of your potential.

Responding to feedback

Training involves being assessed in many areas, including your performance in skills practice where you are observed, receive feedback, are expected to reflect on feedback and revise your approach where needed. This can feel like being judged and escalate a feeling of being criticised, especially when you have a strong inner critic and a history of being criticised. This presents as a potential barrier to development during training as it raises anxiety, reduces self-esteem, and can lead to conflicts with peer and educator relationships. Going forward in time this can be problematic professionally when working with clients if you have a strong critical inner voice making it hard to accept feedback, accept mistakes, and appreciate your growth.

Let us reflect on your current capacity to deal with feedback. Consider the following:

Activity

How do you tend to react to feedback?

Can you allow yourself to hear the feedback before responding?

Can you say you will reflect on the feedback and get back to someone about this later?

Can you recognise areas you need to improve on?
What barriers to hearing feedback are present for you at this time?

Addressing personal barriers through peer support and personal therapy will help to develop a more balanced perspective during training along with the willingness to reframe obstacles as opportunities. Despite this, it can still become hard for people to keep a positive mindset through the demands of high-intensity personal development. The following case study illustrates an example of this.

Case study: Mya

My friend started training a couple of years after I qualified and I tried to support her through her feelings, but she became too critical of herself, the tutor, the assignments, and the course. The opportunities on the course were seen as unrealistic demands that were impossible to achieve. She was negative about the expectations of training and could not accept she needed to look at herself and her reactions differently. Gently challenging her did not work and we ended up falling out when I suggested she may be a little avoidant of the need to come to terms with some of her past. I was sad to see her drop out because she missed the chance to learn so much about herself. She didn't want to start personal therapy yet and found the PD group unsafe and unsupportive. All of that combined became too much for her.

What are the barriers to Mya's development?
What if anything could have helped her to overcome them?
What do you notice about your internal reaction to her?

Sometimes this may have to do with timing. I wonder what else was going on in Mya's life that meant she could not embrace the challenges of training. Psychological safety was not possible and the fear of negative consequences for confronting the expectations of the training was stronger than the capacity for tolerating uncertainty that could lead to personal development. I wonder what her motivations for training were. These hidden aspects are unknown but likely to have set her up with a wall that maintained her sense of safety but was a barrier to development.

Rogers (1959) might call this the functioning of the actualising tendency where the behaviour maintains the self but does not increase the person's potential for growth. Rogers defined the 'actualisng tendency' as 'the inherent tendency of the organism to develop all its capacities in ways which serve to maintain or enhance the organism' (1959, p. 196). For me, Mya was maintaining herself in the best way she could given the circumstances she was in.

She took care of herself, and we should respect that decision in the same way we should respect our clients who decide not to continue therapy.

Reframing problems into opportunities

These are typical problems arising from feeling challenged during training. The reframe offers a way of seeing the potential of the experience to learn and grow and represents a resilient intervention.

Why do we have to do this? > How can I learn from this experience?

I can't do this > What can I do?

I don't have time for all this > What am I choosing to spend my time on?

All the work is coming in at once > What schedule can I work out to fit this in?

There are no placements for me > Who else can I ask about placements?

I don't like being with this person > What do I notice about my reaction?

I don't know if I am any good at this > What evidence do you have that you are bad at this?

I don't feel like anyone is helping me > What help do you need and what are you doing to help yourself?

There is too much to do > What can you do less of?

What if I harm someone? > What if you don't?

I've already had a lot of counselling? > What else could counselling help you with?

This is too much, I can't cope > You are free to leave the course and be proud of how far you have come.

Ponder points

Does any of the above relate to your own experience?
Which ones are particularly difficult for you to reframe?

We can all become stuck in one way of responding and I hope these generate some prompts for discussion with your peers which can increase self-awareness about your reactions. It may also just not be the right time for you to study. Sometimes people decide to leave and worry about whether this is the right or wrong decision. This is a myth. Really, there is no such thing as a right or wrong decision. This is about the need to let go of your previous choice so you can move on to a different path.

Is this the right time to study?

When conditions are favourable there is more of a chance for students to feel safe enough to engage in personal growth. Our sense of safety is impacted by multiple factors such as peer relationships, challenges of groupwork, past experiences of the learning environment such as schooling and assessments, and the trust we have in tutors. Our personal relationships are inevitably impacted by training, and this has been highlighted in a study by Barton (2019) where it was found that some students had left their course 'feeling unable to put in adequate boundaries that would enable them to enjoy 'normal' family life' (Barton, 2019 p. 521). The setting of appropriate boundaries is a key issue arising from the need to section off time for study, and personal reflection something which was also reported in a study by Kennedy and Black (2010) who highlight how counselling students may need to consider setting boundaries with their time and emotional resources to cope with the demands of training for example 'selective investment of personal energy into relationships' (pp. 429–430).

Chapter 13 on self-care considers these issues in more depth encouraging you to pay special attention to your well-being as you are important and you matter too!

Regular attention to any barriers to development can help you along the way as you track your progress through the course requirements. The following activity addresses any barriers such as the timing, interruptions, routines, and support from others.

Activity: Timing

What is the timing like for you?
Is there anything you need to confront now to reduce the impact of wider interruptions to your studies?
Are there any routines you need to alter?
Who can help?
When will you ask them?
Who else can you ask?

Trainee psychotherapist barriers typically experienced during training.

The following table is a list of issues collected from a class activity where the group was asked to consider the typical issues faced as a student in training. The students worked in groups to discuss typical trainee counselling student issues.

Fear	*Comparing self to other*
Imposter Syndrome	*Self-doubt*
Perfectionism	*Disassociation*
Rumination/overthinking	*Work-life balance*
Catastrophising – seeing things as worse than they actually are.	*Social withdrawal*
Comfort eating	*Depression*
Self-sabotage	*Illness*
Avoidance	*Burnout*
Procrastination	

Looking at these may seem overwhelming, but I include these as a way of normalising student vulnerabilities with the hope that you can see this as reassuringly typical and a part of the process. Quite a few of these issues relate to the expectations placed upon oneself especially triggered in response to assessment and other learning tasks such as skills practice, groupwork, presentations, and recording yourself in practice sessions. One way of understanding how you respond to these expectations is through Transactional Analysis theory known as drivers (Kahler, 1975). The Transactional Drivers model can help spot how you react and relate to expectations, raising your self-awareness of a predominant style. These five characteristics have both strengths and weaknesses, for example with a dominant 'be perfect driver' you can set high standards for yourself and achieve these and equally end up doing more than you need to for fear of trusting other people to help achieve the goal.

Take a look at the table below and see what is familiar to you:

Kahler's Drivers

Be strong	Hard to share true feelings, hard to ask for help and concerned about being seen as having a weakness.
Be perfect	The need to be perfect in all you do, find 'ok' not good enough and can be seen as a bit picky
Try hard	See expectations as hard to manage but work really hard draining your energy
Hurry up	Want to rush to the outcome and therefore put pressure on yourself and others to get on with it
Please others	Typically avoids conflict and therefore finds giving and receiving feedback difficult perhaps putting up with things

These drivers are themes you can take to therapy and could help plan your personal development. You might, for example, challenge yourself to ask for a tutorial to examine your fixed ideas about the need to avoid asking for help at all costs.

I remember a student addressing her fear of failure and perfectionism by failing an assignment so that she could let go of the hold this had over her. To help myself with this I similarly submitted an essay knowing it was practically imperfect in every way to let go of my fear of perfectionism I was battling with. I got some excellent feedback and the assessors, knowing my job role as a senior lecturer were more worried about letting me know I had scraped a pass than I was at looking at the mark and areas of development! Below are typical reactions mapped to the drivers for you to muse over. You may be able to spot a couple of these.

Recognising your own drivers. Dare you take a look?

Be strong

You may sit on your worries and try to tackle problems on your own to avoid asking for help. This can mean you come across as self-sufficient and not needing any help. If your feedback is not too good this can shake your self-esteem and frustrate you because you may need to ask for advice on future assignments.

Be perfect

You may avoid starting on a task and procrastinate as a way of avoiding the worry of imperfection. You may also do far more work than is needed before getting started on the assignment as a way of deferring any anxiety about failing. When you are in the midst of researching and writing you may struggle with unhelpful inner dialogue that can get in the way of your progress. If your feedback and mark is not perfect, then you could become defensive questioning the marker or feel devasted and ashamed of your result.

Try hard

You may feel as though everything is so hard and hear yourself complaining about the workload and effort you are putting in. You could be trying so hard that you can't enjoy the learning process. You could feel as though you are suffering so much to meet assignment deadlines and put in excessive amounts of work to get things done. You may expect this to be hard and, in some ways, feel stuck in saying how hard this is and experience a lot of self-doubt about your ability to achieve.

Hurry up

You may look ahead to the whole of the year and want to tackle work way ahead of the deadline asking for pre-course reading, reading for over the summer, and requesting opportunities to hand things in sooner so you can get it done. This can interfere with the enjoyment of learning and prevent you from pacing yourself. It can be stressful for you and underneath this need for quickening things up is anxiety about not being good enough to get it done. You may also question the course design and management of learning because you find it hard to trust the process and schedule that has been planned.

Please others

You may worry about getting it wrong and seek to know 'what do I need to say? What do you want me to do? Is this right?' There could be a lot of self-doubt and self-criticism along the way. You may also defer starting because of this worry and the procrastination here can feel overwhelming to you and to others who are trying to support you. You could feel vulnerable about asking for help too because you don't want to be a burden on anyone else.

Your reactions may be unnoticed by others unless you dare to voice any of this with others. It is really humbling and validating to share these inner struggles and helps the group to know that no one is finding this easy. The success iceberg below is a visual reminder I like to share with groups to facilitate these conversations.

The success iceberg

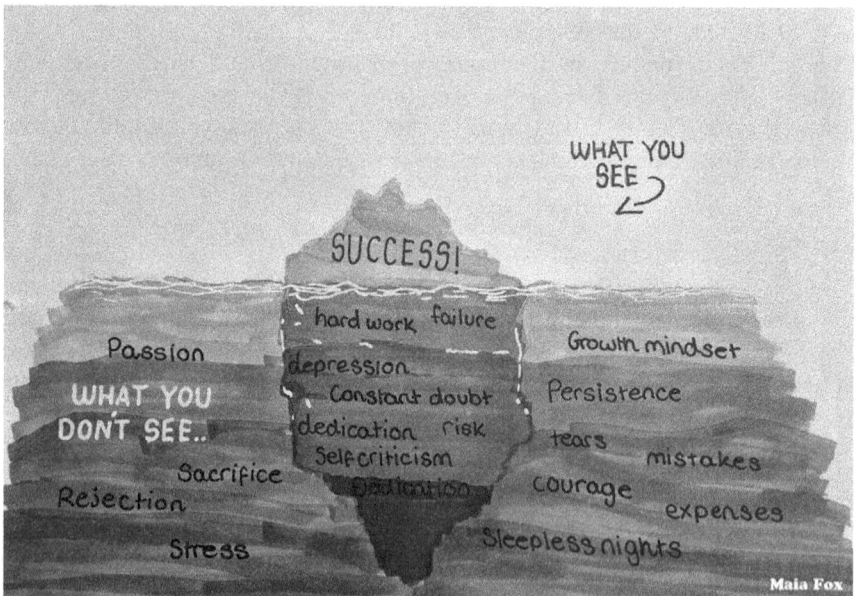

Figure 10.1 The success iceberg
Source: Artwork by Maia Fox.

Success is above the water with the words 'what you see.' Under the water are the words 'what you don't see' and the following words: hard work, failure, depression, constant doubt, dedication, risk, self-criticism, growth mindset, persistence, tears, mistakes, courage, expenses, sleepless nights, passion, sacrifice, rejection and stress.

What we see on the surface as success hides the struggles often unseen underneath such as self-doubt, anxiety, rewriting drafts, reaching out for help with academic writing, learning from feedback, and improving one's style of writing, referencing, and reading. Even those people who get high marks can also go through a process of suffering and self-doubt to meet their perfectionist standards. Yes, some students have developed a competency in academic writing that they can rely on, but they still must set aside time for reading and comprehension, assimilation of concepts to see how ideas relate to each other and are in a process of learning along the way. Lack of effort is a myth, with persistence and perseverance there is success and not knowing what you are doing just yet simply means you are in the process of learning.

Gareth Hughes (2020) explains how students get into anxiety cycles. When anxious they develop poor approaches to study such as procrastination and surface learning resulting in lower scores for their work which feeds into their anxiety about the next assignment that is due.

The cycle then repeats and needs breaking through by improving your study skills including asking for help or studying with others. Working on reframing negative thoughts and developing mindful awareness to increase your attention span can increase your performance in assignments impacting how you see yourself and your capabilities. Developing a growth mindset

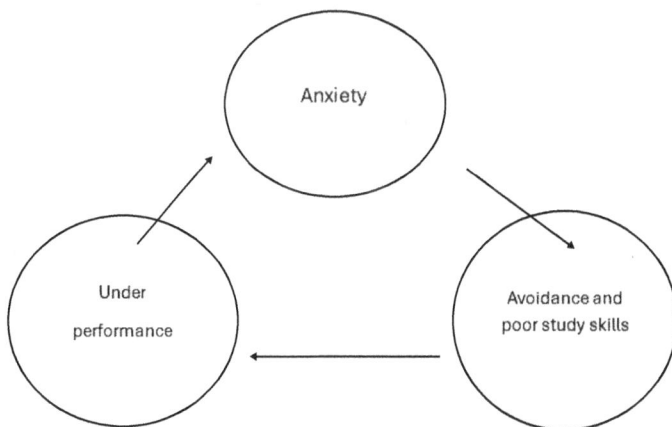

Anxiety Cycles (Hughes, 2020)

Figure 10.2 Anxiety cycles
Source: Hughes, 2020.

(Dweck, 2012) where you are perhaps 'not there yet' along with praising your efforts in learning you can grow from even a failure with a perception shift to seeing this as a FAIL (First Attempt In Learning).

Conclusion

This chapter focuses on your resilient nature and offers promise for growth through addressing barriers. Your reflections on your reactions to training expectations can help you to consider ways to address these. Peers can support each other when feeling overwhelmed and under pressure and tutors appreciate students airing their worries so they can support, reassure, and signpost.

Safe spaces in education may seem like a utopian ideal and it may be more appropriate to call these 'brave spaces' to acknowledge the willingness to have courage, the capacity to embrace challenges, and the self-compassion needed to thrive through your counselling training.

References

Akhtar, S. (2018) Humility. *American Journal Psychoanalysis*, 78, 1–27.

Barton, H. (2019) An exploration of the experiences that counsellors have of taking care of their own mental, emotional and spiritual well-being. *Counselling and Psychotherapy Research*, 20(3), 516–524.

Cleary, R. and Armour, C. (2022) Exploring the role of practitioner lived experience of mental health issues in counselling and psychotherapy. *Counselling Psychotherapy Research*, 22, 1100–1111.

Dweck, C. S. (2012) *Mindset: How You Can Fulfil Your Potential*. London: Constable & Robinson.

Elliott, D. M. and Guy, J. D. (1993) Mental health professionals versus non-mental-health professionals: Childhood trauma and adult functioning. *Professional Psychology: Research and Practice*, 24(1), 83–90.

Hanson, R. (2014) *Hard Wiring Happiness: The New Brain Science of Contentment, Calm and Confidence*. London: Rider.

Hughes, G. (2020) *Be Well Learn Well*. London: Palgrave Macmillan.

Jung, C. G. (1961) *Memories, Dreams and Reflections*. London: Fontana.

Kahler, T. (1975) Scripts: Process and content. *Transactional Analysis Journal*, 5(3), 277–279.

Kennedy, B. S. A. and Black, T. G. (2010) Life outside the 50-minute hour: The personal lives of counsellors. *Canadian Journal of Counselling and Psychotherapy*, 44(4), 421–437.

Neff, K. (2003) Self-compassion: An alternative conceptualization of a healthy attitude toward oneself. *Self and Identity*, 2(2), 85–101.

Online Etymology Dictionary (2024) Capacity (n.). Available from www.etymonline.com/search?q=capacity [date accessed 13 June, 2024].

Ou, A.Y., Tsui, A.S., Kinicki, A.J., Waldman, D.A., Xiao, Z., and Song, L.J. (2014) Humble chief executive officers' connections to top management team integration and middle managers' responses. *Administrative Science Quarterly*, 59, 34–72.

Reivich, K. and Shatté, A. (2002) *The Resilience Factor: 7 Essential Skills for Overcoming Life's Inevitable Obstacles.* New York: Broadway Books.

Richardson, G. E. (1990) The resiliency model. *Health Education*, 21(6), 33–39.

Richardson, G. E. (2002) The metatheory of resilience and resiliency. *Journal of Clinical Psychology*, 58(3), 307–332.

Rogers, C. R. (1959) A theory of therapy, personality and interpersonal relationships as developed in the client-centered framework. In S. Koch (Ed.), *Psychology: A Study of Science* (pp. 184–256). New York: McGraw-Hill.

Segal, Z. V., Williams, J. M. G., and Teasdale, J. D. (2002) *Mindfulness-based Cognitive Therapy for Depression: A New Approach to Preventing Relapse.* London: Guilford Press.

Wax, R., Ranpura, A. and Thubten, G. (2018) *How to be Human: The Manual.* London: Penguin Life.

Chapter 11

First client experience

Jayne Godward

Introduction

Although I have been practising as a counsellor for over 20 years, I can still remember my first client session and how special that was. I can even remember the client and what her issues and life situation were. This was the first step from just practising counselling skills in a classroom or as part of my work to becoming a counsellor. People often describe this as a major milestone in their career. Even though I had been a professional in nursing and teaching with responsibility for others, I found the experience scary, and it felt very different from other roles I had had.

This chapter will explore what going on placement involves and what to expect of this role as you work with a real client for the first time. It will cover:

- the uniqueness of the counselling or therapeutic relationship
- the aspects involved in forming a therapeutic alliance
- the difficulty of emotional involvement
- working ethically within this relationship
- the personal demands of counselling clients
- ideas on setting up and going on placement.

A special kind of relationship

Starting work as a counsellor or psychotherapist is a unique experience. Even if, like me, you had had other professional roles or work supporting people, there are not many occupations where you go into a room with a person you don't know and are expected to make a fairly quick connection with them so that they will tell you about often intimate and personal issues, which they may not have disclosed to anyone else before. Then you are expected to keep these details confidential and not share with others as you would in other team-based occupations. The underpinning factor is confidentiality and although this has its exceptions, it is normally just between the client and counsellor. Compare this to nursing or social work where information would

DOI: 10.4324/9781003405757-12

be shared in a team and notes would be made revealing what the patient/service user had talked about so others could access this. This level of responsibility may seem burdensome; however, you are not holding secrets but maintaining confidentiality which is within safe ethical limits. You do have to keep information to yourself, but you do have a supervisor and a line manager who you can go to for support.

For counselling to be effective, you need to quickly form a relationship with an otherwise unknown person as an unknown other, so that the client feels safe enough to tell you their inner thoughts and feelings or at least start talking about a difficult situation which has brought them to counselling.

The client is likely to be very nervous and anxious about going for counselling and will have certain assumptions about what is going to happen, so first impressions of you will be very important. Do you appear to be friendly, warm and approachable or reserved, uptight and nervous yourself? Somehow you have to project a warmth and a sense of being a safe person to be with.

Case study: Sophia

Sophia is in her mid-30. She has come to your counselling agency for help. She is struggling to concentrate since her recent break-up with her partner, Jade and the loss she feels. Jade was the love of her life, and she says that she is heart-broken.

Sophia has been allocated to you as her situation is less complex than some of the other clients who are on the waiting list.

Question: What will you do to create a safe space for Sophia? What will you do to start to create a connection during this first session?

Personal considerations

Before we look at possible answers to this case study, it is important to explore what might be going on for you as a trainee but also any of us when we have a new client. There is likely to be some nervousness and a degree of anxiety which might go along the lines of:

- Will I be able to connect with this person?
- Will I be good enough or able to work with their issues?
- Do I have enough knowledge and skills?
- Will I be able to help?
- Will they like me?
- Will differences get in the way? E.g., in my case, I am a co-habiting, older, heterosexual woman whilst Sophia is a gay woman who has no longer got her partner and is nearly half my age. How might she see me? Will there be barriers to connection here? Will I struggle to empathise with her?

One trainee said:

> My first client experience felt like an overwhelming giant that I had to conquer. The premise of sitting with a person, someone you have never met before and cannot put a face to, allowing you to be with them baring all their inner vulnerabilities felt unimaginable.
>
> Nevertheless, on the day of my first session a strange calm came over me and an understanding that today was the day and that after all of the training I have received it was time for me to be present and show up. Not only physically but metaphorically, I had a responsibility to be there for the person seeking help.
>
> The feelings of nervousness faded as I knew I had a job to do. I greeted my client, a two-way instant respect was established. As the session began and the contracting was finished, I thought to myself that I had made this happen and this is what I want for a career. The discussion blew me away as I realised what an honour it was to be trusted with such delicate issues. After leaving the session the feeling of euphoria made every feeling of nervousness worth it, I will never look back.

Anxiety or nerves before seeing a new client is common for most therapists at all stages in their careers. I think it is useful as it guards against complacency and helps us to reflect on what might be required. Each client is unique, and each counselling relationship is different.

There has been some interesting research into therapist self-doubt, particularly at the start of therapy which has been linked to better client outcomes (see Brown, 2023; Theriaut, Gazzola and Richardson, 2009; Odyniec et al, 2019).

So having some self-doubt or feelings of incompetence are both normal and can be useful. Brown (2023) found that it helped keep therapists more open, sensitive and reflexive when they started the therapeutic work, whilst the relationship was developing.

In a study of novice counsellors, it was found that what mattered to the client was the counsellor's relational persona and their human qualities rather than their specific orientation or interventions (De Stefano et al., 2010). So there is something here about being yourself and being human. Not being too worried that you are a trainee.

Ponder points

What can you rely on about yourself?
What qualities do you have already which you can trust and depend upon when you enter the counselling relationship?

In the next anecdote the student uses their resources and knowledge to help them through the first session:

> Before beginning placement, I felt ready to progress from peer skills sessions to something less formulaic and more authentic. But as I read through the file for my first client, the weight of responsibility felt immense and seeds of self-doubt crept in. Was I ready? It reminded of the panic I felt being told I could take my firstborn home from hospital.
>
> I concentrated on deep breathing and repeated the core conditions in my head. I felt anxiety as sat down to talk through the contract and CORE-10 form. But as the minutes passed, my nerves dissipated, and empathic focus took over. Fear or worry cropped up at times when I became too aware of specific interventions – was that a closed question... did I just miss a chance to explore emotion?
>
> I felt all sorts of emotions on the drive home – elation for making it through the session with no major blunders, privileged that the client shared feelings they had never discussed with anyone else, but also a deep sadness for the client and their current struggles. The following day, the emotional intensity diminished, replaced by a sense of awe for this opportunity and an increased confidence in my abilities.

Forming a therapeutic relationship

Unlike other professional or helping work where we 'do unto' a person, we are aiming to form a trusting relationship where the client has the space to do the exploring that they need to do. Counsellors and psychotherapists may use techniques in their work depending on their approach, but the connection and working alliance is still required.

Goldfried and Eubanks (2019) stress the importance of developing a good enough relationship with the client so that collaboration can take place and facilitating the therapeutic alliance is seen as one of the important principles of change (see Wotton and Johnston, 2022).

Here I believe that to form this alliance, the six therapeutic conditions of Carl Rogers, the founder of Person-Centred Theory are still required even if you are not a Person-Centred trainee and are studying to offer integrative, psychodynamic or more solution focussed interventions. These are as follows:

1   Two persons are in contact
2   The first person, whom we shall term the client, is in a state of incongruence being vulnerable, or anxious
3   That the second person, whom we shall term the therapist, is congruent in the relationship
4   The therapist is experiencing unconditional positive regard towards the client

5   That the therapist is experiencing empathic understanding of the client's internal frame of reference
6   That the client perceives, at least to a minimal degree, conditions 4 and 5, the unconditional positive regard of the therapist for him, and the empathic understanding of the therapist (Reeves, 2022, p. 66).

So, the aim is to make a connection with Sophia, our case study client and to work with her to help her to explore her situation and discuss her feelings of loss. This cannot be done if there is no psychological contact between you.

Tolan says, 'Psychological contact is a mutual thing. Each person must receive the other; I must know that you are here, and you must know that I am here' (Tolan, 2012, p. 84).

In her book, Tolan (2012) explores both basic, cognitive and subtle psychological contact. She talks about the client's availability for making basic contact and the barriers to this and looks at the skills for establishing contact which include the skills you will learn or will have learned on counselling skills courses. Hopefully you will come to your first sessions ready to receive your client and be prepared to be present for them and give them space. But there are times when we are all distracted, and this interrupts the contact and the presence we have.

Similarly, clients may lose concentration and may seem psychologically distant from you at times when they are accessing deeper emotions, or are anxious about things outside the counselling room or distracted by incoming phone messages. There is more possibility for distractions and interruptions to contact working remotely with clients on a Zoom or a Teams call or working on the telephone when they are in their own homes, and you are in yours.

As a therapist, it is important to be grounded and to be able to leave your own anxieties and worries and the general busyness of the day behind when you enter the counselling space.

One trainee, L, described running into her agency, having dropped her small baby off at a relative's house. Her client was already there and there was very little time for her to calm down before needing to invite the person into the counselling room. It is likely that L was still dealing with the emotions of leaving her baby with a relative. Had a beating heart and state of tension having rushed in and was not fully present for her client when she went to collect her from the waiting area.

If there is contact and a basic rapport is created, then the relationship has begun and the client is more likely to come back and you will be starting your work as a counsellor, however, there are times when even if the first session has seemed satisfactory, the client may choose not to come back for personal or circumstantial reasons. For some clients, just telling their story might be enough. For others they may have dipped their toe in the water and have started to talk about something difficult then have decided it is too painful to go there. For others, there might be a fear of intimacy having felt the presence of the therapist but maybe not being able to cope with this. Not everyone wants a relationship! Counselling or psychotherapy is not for everyone! So don't be too hard on yourself if any of your clients do not come back or if they attend for a few sessions then stop coming. See Bernstein (2021) for reasons why clients don't return.

On the other hand, sometimes it may be enough for someone to come and air what is on their mind and then they may not return. There is quite a bit of literature written about single session therapy (see Cameron, 2007; Jackson, 2020).

Realistically, however competent your skills and however interpersonally adept you are, you just might not be the right person for them. We explore this a bit more in Chapter 15 when we look at personal therapy.

Ponder points

Think about times you have been listening to others. This can be in your work setting, supporting others or with friends and family.
What stopped you giving them your full attention and being present to them?

Difficulty of emotional involvement

Imagine that you have been asked to work with Sophia, in the case study. How might her situation trigger feelings in you due to your own history? What might you be tempted to do or say to help her?

It might be that even during your first session you start to become emotionally involved or as the counselling develops.

What do we mean by emotional involvement?

The problem here is that you are aiming to form a good relationship with your client and this will involve empathising with her situation but with that can come degrees of emotional involvement. This could vary between feeling a genuine caring or warmth for the person, to feeling anxious about their predicament or even becoming distressed if the client reveals something harrowing or painful. As we enter the internal frame of reference or worlds of our client's and listen to their feelings we may be affected by disturbing or grim details. In Chapter 13 we examine how you can develop self-kindness and self-compassion to attend to your self-care.

Normally as a new trainee you wouldn't be expected to work with clients who are traumatised or suicidal but sometimes it may not be apparent at the time of assessment and as you build a relationship with a person, they may share these feelings.

Another way in which you might become overly involved is because you really like your client and start to overidentify with them and really want to help.

Case study: Mark and Ben

Mark is a new trainee, he has been working with his first client, Ben at a youth counselling service. They have built up a good rapport and Ben has been looking at ways that he can deal with the effects of bullying he experienced at school which previously made him miserable and ill. Gradually he is building is self-confidence through the therapeutic work. Mark is reminded of a horrible time he had at college where he was picked on and felt suicidal as a result. He really wants to help Ben feel better but also fears for him due to his own experience.

Ben does not turn up for his fifth session and does not let Mark know via the administrator. Mark is very worried. He immediately thinks Ben might have harmed himself or made an attempt on his life. That night he cannot sleep and is taken back to the day when he nearly threw himself under a train because he felt so low. He wonders if he should ring Ben or try to find his address and go around to see him, as he knows he lives locally.

Luckily the next day, Mark decides to contact his supervisor and is able to talk through his fears. The supervisor is calm and logical, she recognises that Mark was concerned but does not feel Ben is particularly at risk. In the meantime, the next day, Mark finds out that Ben did contact his agency to let them know he would not be attending due to an exam resit, unfortunately the administrator had been off sick, so the message had not been sent on to him.

This shows that overinvolvement is possible, particularly if you overidentify with a client's situation and are triggered by what they are bringing. Triggers are not unusual when working with clients. I am amazed how often I have sat down with a client and they have talked about an issue which has resonated with something personal in my own life.

I would like to point out here that overidentifying or becoming over-involved with a client is not the same as empathising and may become a barrier to empathy because you are in your own frame of reference and are not seeing matters from the client's perspective. Instead of empathy, you may also be showing sympathy and feel sorry for this client. This could actually cause difficulties in the relationship and be harmful to the client. It might mean you step over the line into wanting help them in more practical ways, e.g., giving advice or suggesting a solution to their problem.

Another reason for emotional involvement might be if you experience transference towards your client. Simply transference is when the other person reminds you of someone in your past or present life and this leads to you treating them or reacting to them as if they were this person (see Short and Thomas, 2015). For example, if a client reminds you of an elderly relative and you start to treat that person as if they were that person and are no longer seeing them as the person they are.

Working ethically

Here it might be useful to remind you of some ethical principles. The BACP identify six ethical principles which you can carry around in your pocket to help keep you focussed. These are being trustworthy, autonomy, beneficence, non-maleficence, justice and self-respect (BACP, 2018).

In the case of the elderly client who reminds you of a relative, there might be a danger of you taking over and doing more for the client than you would normally, reducing their *autonomy, their right to self-govern* and also treating them more favourably than other clients (*justice*, the fair and impartial treatment of all clients).

If we look at the case study of Ben and Mark. Mark has proved himself *to be trustworthy* and has attended sessions with Ben on time and has kept his client's confidentiality even when he had concerns. A good relationship was formed where he provided a safe space for Ben to talk.

Mark struggled with respecting Ben's *autonomy, his right to self-govern* when he became overinvolved and nearly took action which wasn't necessary as the evidence that the client would take his own life was meagre and based on Mark's past experience.

Ben had been benefitting (*beneficence*) from having the space to talk about the bullying he suffered and the effects and is starting to build his self-esteem. As a result he had taken steps to resit the exams he failed in school. Mark nearly fractured the relationship by becoming over involved emotionally.

Mark was concerned that his client might come to harm and wanted to prevent this (*non-maleficence*) however, he nearly caused harm by wanting to rush to rescue the client and cross the boundaries of the relationship by ringing Ben up or even going to his house.

There would also have been a lack of *justice* here, firstly by not treating Ben as an individual and respecting his rights and also because it is unlikely that Mark would do this with all his clients.

Luckily, Mark contacted his supervisor and was able to talk about his triggers to that person and his anxieties and fears were eased. This fits with the principle of *self-respect* which involves care of self. His supervisor also identified a need for personal therapy.

These examples show that it is essential that any decisions you take are weighed up using the ethical principles as guides.

Personal demands

Don't underestimate the personal demands of going on placement and seeing your first clients. You are entering into the emotional worlds of individuals who are, usually, in some kind of distress. You are trying to understand feelings and experiences which may involve some kind of trauma. Like Mark in the case study, you might be impacted due to overidentification, or you may just feel really sad or upset by what you are hearing. You need to be prepared for this and have your support network ready.

It is good practice to have your individual supervision in place prior to starting client work. I see this as the trainee having a safe base from which to work. If you have already met with your supervisor and feel that you have started to form a relationship where you can bring any issues, it will feel easier to go and work with your first clients. Who are you going to speak to, if in the worst-case scenario, things go wrong in your first therapy session? You might not want to talk to the agency manager, or this might not be appropriate.

Also meeting with your new supervisor prior to the start of counselling work, means you can check out questions which you are unsure of in a safe space without feeling foolish (e.g., how to contract with the client, what to wear, discuss the referral you have been given, really look at your hopes and fears for the counselling work). We look at supervision in more detail in Chapter 14.

The authors of this book also recommend that students have personal therapy during their training and perhaps before or during client work as we believe that this helps to develop self-awareness and emotional resilience when engaging in this work. It is a way of dealing with potential triggers or issue which arise for us as we work with clients. Working with clients is always a journey into the unknown for us, so we need to be as prepared as possible, whilst acknowledging that we need to be able to deal with unpredictability in the counselling work.

Unrealistic expectations

Sometimes our unpreparedness is linked to unrealistic expectations of how a placement or client work is going to be.

I asked a placement manager, "What are some of the unrealistic expectations students have?"

She said:

- That clients behave in session like in skills practice!
- That they will be able to use their well-polished skills when often all they do is sit with the client in their pain.
- That clients want to work on the root of their issues when actually they just want to feel better today!

Activity: Dealing with the unexpected

Consider these situations:

- What if your client wants you to hold their hand or hug them?
- What if your client bursts into tears? How would you feel?
- Their mobile phone goes off and they answer.

- Your client comes in and will not take their coat off.
- Your client has strong body odour.
- Your client comes in and gets out and starts eating a sandwich.
- On a Zoom call, the person's partner /child comes into the room.

All these are potential scenarios which can happen with clients. You might want to discuss these with your supervisor or in your training group before you start.

Principally, the way you respond to a client needs to contain an underlying respect and empathy for them and be informed by your ethical framework.

Setting up and going on placement

In my experience as a counselling tutor, one of the hardest tasks can be finding a placement. On most undergraduate or post-graduate courses you are expected to find your own agency. Some training organisations have their own placement units or designated tutors to help you but there is some effort required on your part to search out and contact appropriate organisation. Availability will vary according to where you live and the demand, for example in a small town it may be limited but even in a big city, it may difficult if there are a lot of counselling training courses with students vying for places.

I asked two very experienced placement managers about their experiences working with students on placement and I have incorporated some of their replies into this section. I will call them Linda and Julie.

You need to be as flexible as possible about the days and times you can offer. This is often difficult if a student is working full-time and has only evenings or weekends available.

Before you apply to a placement, Linda said:

> I feel it is imperative that students understand what is expected of them regarding policies and procedures and how they fit with the ethos of the organisation. Students should research their chosen placement to ensure it fits with the perspective underpinning their training. Areas of commonality of interest help both parties develop rapport due to a shared value base.

You will find it easier to get a placement if you have already been doing voluntary or paid work supporting vulnerable people or have held a position of trust. Even so, you need to be prepared to sell yourself and promote your unique abilities as you may be in competition with others with professional experience. As I advised in Chapter 3, you will need to show your positive personal qualities in your application to placements.

Although you may feel that you are helping the placement provide a service and they should be grateful for your services. Linda said:

> Charitable organisations have considerable tensions around funding and resource availability and having students on placement costs a lot in time training and support.

So, agencies are looking for people who they will be able to trust and those who will use their initiative and will bring a level of professionalism so that they don't need too much support.

I asked Julie, a manager of a large placement, what they look for in students. She said:

> I look for students that are well processed, that have a good level of awareness of what their trigger points may be and how they will manage this in session. I am always interested in what has bought them to a potential career in counselling and how they deliver the answer to this question in interview, it needs to be congruent not rehearsed! For me, especially with CPCAB level 4 students, it is what they do outside their formal learning to build their knowledge and fundamentally their practice, I want to know what CPD they are doing, what podcasts they are listening to and what books they are reading.

She also recommended the need for good communication as the placement progresses:

> As learning progresses and students develop proficiencies, they will benefit from openly communicating concerns through line management and where possible through discussion with their assigned mentor and their clinical supervisor to reduce the possibility of conflict and to be able to be flexible in responding to organisational stresses.

To sum up, to acquire a placement you need to show a level of confidence and determination and may have to be assertive, by keeping on contacting people, as the placement manager will be a very busy person who may not get back to you straight away or may be inundated with mails from prospective students. You need to stand out in what you can offer and, in really show your interest in working at that organisation. The more flexible you are in terms of availability, the better your chances. Remember the placement will not work around you and will see themselves as offering you an opportunity rather than seeing you as the opportunity!

Conclusion

This chapter has aimed to give you a flavour of what starting work with clients involves and an understanding of the demands of working therapeutically with others. The therapeutic relationship is unique and unlike many other types of helping. We have explored creating this and what the demands of working within this involve. I have touched on the requirements of going on placement and have sought the opinions of placement managers to support this. I hope that I have helped towards your preparation for this important part of counselling and therapy training.

References

BACP (2018) *Ethical Framework for the Counselling Professions*. Lutterworth: BACP.

Bernstein, F. (2021) Understanding why clients drop out. *Therapy Today*, 32(7), 35.

Brown, S. (2023) Dealing with the demon doubt. *Therapy Today*, 34(2), 26.

Cameron, C. L. (2007) Single session and walk-in psychotherapy: A descriptive account of the literature. *Counselling and Psychotherapy Research*, 7(4), 245–249.

De Stefano, J., Mann-Feder, V., and Gazzola, N. (2010) A qualitative study of client experiences of working with novice counsellors. *CPR*, 10(2), 139–146.

Goldfried, M. and Eubanks, C. F. (2019) A principle-based approach to psychotherapy integration. In Norcross, J. and Goldfried, M. (Eds), *Handbook of Psychotherapy Integration*, 3rd edn. Oxford University Press.

Jackson, C. (2020) The big interview; 'Not all clients need or want a deep relationship with their counsellors'. *Therapy Today*, 31(6), 24.

Odyniec, P., Probst, T., Margraf, J., and Willutzki, U. (2019) Psychotherapist trainees' professional self-doubt and negative personal reaction: Changes during cognitive behavioral therapy and association with patient progress. *Psychotherapy Research: Journal of the Society for Psychotherapy Research*, 29(1), 123–138.

Reeves, A. (2022) *An Introduction to Counselling and Psychotherapy*. London: Sage.

Short, F. and Thomas, P. (2015) *Core Approaches in Counselling and Psychotherapy*. London: Routledge.

Theriault, A, Gazzola, N., and Richardson, B. (2009) Feelings of incompetence in novice therapists: consequences, coping and correctives. *Canadian Journal of Counselling and Psychotherapy*, 43(2), 105–119.

Tolan, J. (2012) *Skills in Person-Centred Counselling and Psychotherapy*. London: Sage.

Wotton, M. and Johnston, G. (2022) We need more faith that therapy works. *Therapy Today*, 33(2), 25.

Chapter 12

The world in the counselling room

Tara Fox and Jayne Godward

Counselling or therapy could be seen as just a one-to-one activity or one done with couples that takes place in a private space away from the rest of the world. Client issues could be seen as individual issues rather than a result of wider societal and worldwide problems.

This chapter aims to turn this view upside down and look at the impact that our society and the world we live in has on clients and their counsellors.

We explore some of the issues that clients bring into the room and to a lesser extent what counsellors bring in.

We will focus briefly on structural inequality, the impact of social media, climate change, the legacy of the Covid-19 Pandemic and world conflict and political unrest

It is impossible to look in detail at each of these topics, but the purpose is to raise your awareness as a would-be counsellor to the importance of keeping your work within a worldwide and societal perspective and helping you consider the difficulty of doing work with individuals when their issues may be a symptom of living in our current society. It is hoped that you will do further reading or training to increase your knowledge of these areas.

In this chapter, we will look at:

- therapists' views: the worldwide and societal issues which enter the counselling room
- the impact of structural inequality and discrimination
- the influence of social media usage on clients
- climate change and anxiety
- the effects of the pandemic
- working in an unsettled global environment
- the circle of influence and control.

DOI: 10.4324/9781003405757-13

Experiences of therapists

Ponder points

What kinds of societal and worldwide issues do you think clients and counsellors bring into the counselling room?
List as many issues as you can think of.

We were interested to know what other practitioners thought were the wider societal issues which affected both clients and counsellors. We sent a short survey out to different people within our network of therapists. Eight different therapists replied in answer to our questions. The key question was:

Can you briefly list the wider societal and worldwide issues which have come up in the counselling room?

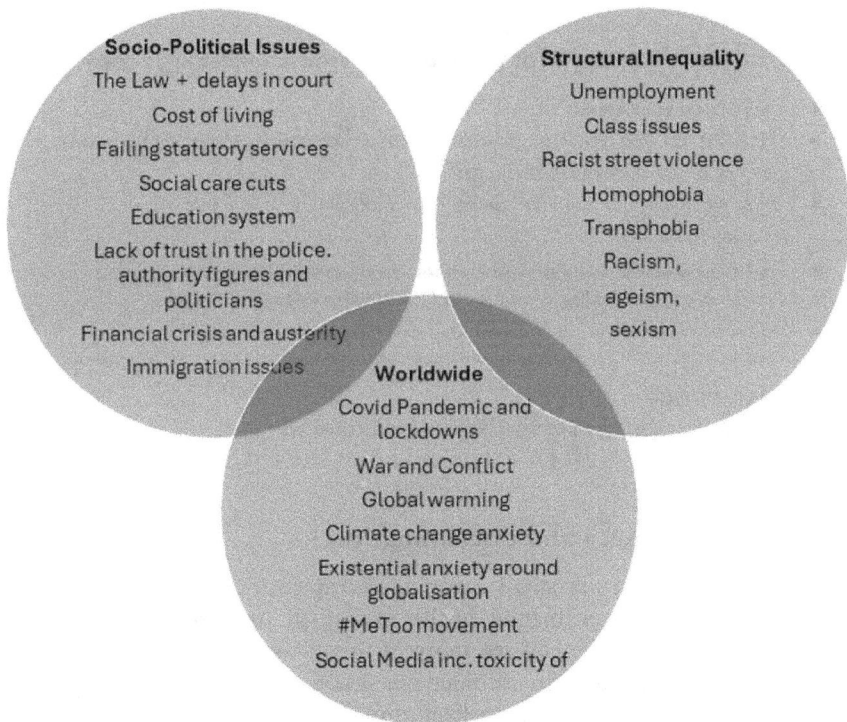

Socio-Political Issues
The Law + delays in court
Cost of living
Failing statutory services
Social care cuts
Education system
Lack of trust in the police, authority figures and politicians
Financial crisis and austerity
Immigration issues

Structural Inequality
Unemployment
Class issues
Racist street violence
Homophobia
Transphobia
Racism,
ageism,
sexism

Worldwide
Covid Pandemic and lockdowns
War and Conflict
Global warming
Climate change anxiety
Existential anxiety around globalisation
#MeToo movement
Social Media inc. toxicity of

Issues which clients brought into the counselling room

Figure 12.1 Issues which clients brought into the counselling room

We also asked for examples of how clients were affected by specific issues which we have included, if relevant, later in the sections of this chapter.

It was difficult to categorise the issues which were cited. In a rough fashion I have divided these areas into *socio-political, structural inequality* and *worldwide*.

Socio-political relates to the way a country is governed in terms of priorities and funding for different services and the way this affects our clients.

Structural inequality recognises the discrimination embedded in our society and our culture and relates directly to the issues which clients might bring to counselling because of the minority or socio-economic group they belong to.

Finally, the *worldwide* issues category is about issues which affect people in our world either directly or indirectly and may cause our clients incredible anxiety.

My diagram recognises an overlap between these as individual countries and Governments are impacted by worldwide events and cannot operate in isolation from the rest of the world.

Before we focus on some specific areas, it may be useful for you to think about working within a worldwide and societal context within the counselling room using the questions below.

In practice: Working with the world in your counselling room

- What are your views?
- How far do you think worldwide issues or societal issues unite us with our clients or do they cause divisions?
- Are we joined by anxiety? Does this underpin how we feel about a lot of worldwide issues?
- How does a counsellor maintain hope during pessimistic times?
- What is the counsellor's role during difficult or turbulent times?
- How can we stay grounded and help our clients stay grounded?
- What do we as counsellors need to do to prevent ourselves being overwhelmed?
- Should therapists be political? What action could we take?

Structural inequality and discrimination

As we have seen from our small survey of therapists, our clients may present with concerns and poor mental health arising in part from systemic and structural oppression. We can see more of this if we shift our view of client presenting issues outwards to consider the structural harm in society such as unemployment or marginalisation from dominant groups or abuse of power. Campbell, Tamasese and Waldergrave (2001) point out how client issues can be traced back to these structures and yet they may blame themselves for their own suffering for example stress and burnout may be internalised and experienced as 'I am not good enough' or 'I am not worthy.' Being more aware of the effects of structural oppression can open up the counselling room so that therapists may challenge the way individuals take personal blame for their own suffering.

The medical profession diagnoses individuals, further exacerbating the personal blame arising from the labelling of mental health conditions, as could happen with eco-anxiety which we will look at later. Although labels can be helpful at times to locate a reason for the way people feel, it can also lead people to self-blame rather than perceiving their suffering as a reaction to the context they are in.

Therapists work with individuals and offer tailored support to meet the needs of the person, but this should not leave out consideration of the environment and wider societal influences on mental health and wellbeing. The following case study shows how the wider issues including faith, identity, culture and organisational issues combine to trigger mental health issues.

Case study: Coleen

Coleen is a Christian woman of Caribbean heritage who works as a nurse in a cancer charity. She works long hours and although she enjoys caring for patients and supporting families, she feels drained. The organisation is short-staffed, and she feels it is her duty as a good Christian and a nurse to help. The extra shifts are making her feel increasingly tired and her mood is low. Staff often call in sick at the last minute and Coleen is really aware of the impact on patients if good care is not on hand. She feels stressed, tired and has been diagnosed with depression. Coleen feels she is letting herself down by not coping with the role. She says she is ashamed to be depressed and asks, 'where is God when I need him?' She expresses that she feels unworthy of Gods help and not good enough as a nurse. She has been signed off as sick from work for a month and says she feels wretched.

If we consider counselling to be an individual practice, then we may miss multiple levels of understanding that can be gained from considering the person in context.

Contemporary approaches to counselling encourage the development of socially justice-centred practice which involves seeking to provide equitable services and support for all people with the understanding that identity is socially constructed (Lee and Humphrey, 2023). Below you are invited to open up your understanding of the client's issues by using different lenses.

Activity: Coleen

When you read about Coleen's presenting issues what do you notice if you look at this case through the following lenses?

- Gender
- Race
- Power
- Faith
- Oppression
- Organisational structure and culture

There are cross-cultural lenses to consider here around the role of nursing, caring responsibilities, and of teamwork. Coleen's faith identity is also an influencing factor in her suffering but so is the organisation's structure and culture. Reflecting on Coleen's multiple identities and structural factors extends your view of the client's presenting issues to include the wider world.

The influence of social media in the counselling room

Many people enjoy the benefits of social media blending their online and offline lives through a sense of 'connected presence' (Licoppe, 2004). Boundaries have extended so much that it is no longer relevant to see a distinction between 'real life' and 'online life.' This is especially the case for younger people many of whom would feel cut off from their life without this access to the people and groups where they feel a sense of connection and belonging. Many practitioners now include a question about social media usage at the assessment and I see this as a positive change that recognises the significance of its nature and likely impact in the counselling room.

The social media self however represents what we choose to show and reveal to the world. For some this can be an inauthentic representation of living the good life impacting social media user's confidence levels when we compare ourselves to others.

Therapist perspectives

From our short survey therapists reported wider societal issues affecting their clients:

THERAPIST 1: Social media – it has had a real impact on self-esteem, how they measure success, their expectations of life, and assumptions about the success of others.

This can be frustrating to hear about as it seems all consuming for the client and an overpowering influence from the wider world that can be challenging to work with in the therapy room:

THERAPIST 1: [continues] As someone who had the 'luxury' of being a young person and young adult in an era when social media did not exist, I found the impact it was having on my client disturbing. It also made me feel very angry on their behalf because social media can be switched off but the pressure to be on it is immense and it is a construct that is neither social nor media. Lives are being affected because others are projecting successful lives that they don't really have and other people are measuring themselves against these false claims.

Adding further to the trends in comparing oneself to others I have noticed how clients use the language of social media to communicate about their health issues using language such as 'I have daddy issues' or 'I have such awful FOMO.' This shows how people reflect on their mental health when using social media but this can cause problems if people begin to self-diagnose without seeking appropriate help. There are powerful influencers who impact on beliefs and attitudes of their followers. Heteronormativity (a worldview that populates heterosexuality as normal or preferred) and sexism for example are promoted online and microaggressions chip away at confidence in identity development:

THERAPIST 2: A Young woman being treated with contempt by boyfriend. She struggled to take issue with such powerful influencers, kept thinking she must be wrong. Was stuck for a while looking for her mistake.
THERAPIST 3: Empathising and exploring heteronormativity has helped to build our working alliance … my client didn't know how to be single and gay in a world that has changed. We are now working together on finding her own identity as a newly single gay young woman.

The development of our identity is especially hard when we are in the adolescent stage and our attention centres on our identity versus role confusion (Erikson, 1950). Teenagers may feel conflicted and experiment with different roles to see where they fit in society on the road to developing their sense of self. A recent literature review explores adolescent perspectives on social media and mental health (Popat and Tarrant, 2023) identifying five themes:

1   self-expression and validation,
2   appearance comparison and body ideals,
3   pressure to stay connected,
4   social engagement and peer support,
5   exposure to bullying and harmful content.

The authors also raise how distressing news in the world accompanied by violent graphic images can cause intrusive thoughts and nightmares.

Harmful content

Working in the field of mental health we need to be aware of social media usage and raise awareness of the necessity of protecting the 'self' online from such harmful content. Such news feeds can be triggering for those who have lived experience of these issues, leading to re-traumatisation (Scott et al., 2023). We rarely hyper-fixate on the good stuff which would bring us more of the same.

Neuroscientists have explained how our brains have a negativity bias and are programmed to look for the bad stuff in order to keep us safe from harm (see Larsen, Smith and Cacioppo's study (1998) which found that negative information 'weighs more heavily on the brain' (pp. 887–900)). Increasing news feeds affects our mood as our choice of focus grows more results. The more people look into a topic, the more of the same material is generated on their social media platforms increasing the impact on them.

High-profile stories containing harmful content spread fast thus 'go viral' exposing social media users to words, images and stories of a distressing nature. Coming into contact with traumatic content in the media (e.g., world conflicts, and devastation due to climate change) has been found to activate the fear response in the brain leading to psychological and physical distress (Johnston and Davey, 1997). We will be looking more at the effects in later sections of this chapter.

Climate change

The issue

Climate change is not a new issue. People were aware of climate change and its possible effects over 40 years ago (Reese, Swank and Sturm, 2023). An emergency was first declared in 2019 with the first world climate conference taking place.

We are now seeing environmental destruction occurring including melting ice caps, the loss of rainforests, wildfires, flooding, a decline in insect life and different species of wildlife. Previously it might have been seen as something far away but in recent years, we have seen it closer to home (Aspey, 2021).

Aspey talks about the idea of the 'protected bubble' of the counselling room when the destruction of the world is outside and quotes Yasmin Kapadia, 'there will be no therapy on a dead planet' (Aspey, 2021).

We have already looked at structural inequality and yet again, those who are most likely to be affected by climate change are those who are most disadvantaged, e.g., the elderly, poor, children and those of low socio-economic status as well as those in minority racial and ethnic groups and those with disabilities. These groups already have less power in society and therefore will have fewer means to cope with the effects of climate change (Reese, Swank and Sturm, 2023).

The effects on clients

In his report on climate anxiety, Pihkala (2019) says this may cause the person to feel paralysed, but this can be seen as an understandable reaction to the massive problem climate change poses. Climate anxiety is part of a wider phenomenon called eco-anxiety which includes a range of emotions.

Pihkala (2019 p. 8) divides this into two categories – severe psychosomatic and milder symptoms:

> If someone is severely affected, they can suffer insomnia, states of depression, difficulty in maintaining functioning when faced with news about climate change and its consequences and the threat as well as compulsive behaviour. Someone who is severely affected may adopt self-destructive behaviours including substance abuse and self-harm.
>
> Milder symptoms of climate anxiety include insomnia, sadness, temporary paralysis (e.g., not knowing what to do), mood effects. The researchers found that media reports directly affect stress.

The vulnerability of a client will depend on the person's history and personality traits. The most vulnerable people are children and teenagers and young people who are already struggling with MH issues. People who live close to nature and have a strong bond to eco-systems will of course be most affected, e.g., those working on the land or reliant on the land or the environment for their livelihoods (Pihkala, 2019).

A recent survey of 10,000 people across ten countries aged 16–25 found 60% of young people feel worried or extremely worried. Two thirds felt sad, afraid and anxious. Four out of ten felt betrayed, ignored and abandoned by politicians and adults (Aspey, 2021).

Global studies have shown that 84% of young people are at least moderately worried about climate change with half reporting that these feelings negatively affect their daily lives and functioning. It was felt that there was an inadequate government response to the issue and a sense of betrayal (Hickman, Marks and Pihkala, 2021).

In an Australian study (Silva and Coburn, 2023), therapists reported a change of attitude in young people to concerns about safety and resources rather than them having aspirations for the future.

As climate change increasingly affects all of us it is predicted that there will be a sharp rise in mental health issues in the coming years, as a result counsellors and therapists are going to be working with these issues in their counselling rooms. So, we look briefly at what might be required below.

The counselling response: How to work with clients

In Silver and Coburn's study (2023), the therapists interviewed felt unsettled and frustrated due to feeling complicit in the problem of the climate crisis and its making. They were aware of the human damage which had been caused whilst feeling that they had good intentions. There was a tension between knowing and doing and a foreboding that something terrible was coming. They felt that professional bodies were not attending to the climate crisis issue and slow to recognise its importance.

This study emphasised the need for therapists to pay attention to their existential concerns and unconscious processes and be aware of these processes existing in parallel with those of clients.

In a similar vein, Nick Totton, (BACP 2021), a psychotherapist and ecopsychologist, talks about a tendency for therapists to ignore and deny the reality of climate change and the need for them to acknowledge their fear and feelings of helplessness to clients, if necessary, then to encourage them to explore how it is for them. Here there is a sense of being alongside clients rather than pathologising them or treating them as a person with a problem when climate change is an issue which unites us all and is not to be treated as a mental health issue. Here anxiety is a healthy response to a serious crisis and what would be unhealthy is deny this.

Pihkala (2019) says this anxiety can be a resource if people have the time and space to deal with their emotions and then start to take part in constructive activities to mitigate the destruction which has already been caused.

Seth et al. (2023) recommend a trauma-informed and person-centred approach where the person's unique circumstances, experiences and identities are understood and where the therapist is aware of their own knowledge, values and biases when assisting clients with their distress.

This section has stressed the need for counsellors to gain more understanding of this issue and to attend to their reactions to this crisis prior to working alongside clients who also need to explore how this issue is affecting them. We hope that you will read some of the research and articles cited here to enrich your knowledge.

The Covid pandemic

The Covid-19 pandemic is another powerful example of how the world entered the counselling room. The Pandemic had a massive impact on people across the UK and across the world.

As the pandemic spread and more people started to be affected and die from it, governments in the UK and other countries responded by bringing in laws imposing social isolation and lockdowns. March 2020 saw the first lockdown in the UK where socialising started to be restricted and going out to work was discouraged then forbidden where possible. Everyone's lives were affected and most of us suffered an increase in our anxiety levels. There was an underlying fear of catching the virus and of dying from it. During the height of the pandemic, the UK Government gave daily briefings and the figures of people with Covid-19 and the deaths toll.

According to a recent report by the Centre for Mental Health which analysed data from different studies, 62% of people felt anxious and worried at the onset of the pandemic and two in five people experienced the likely symptoms of depression and anxiety with one in ten people reporting suicidal feelings (Duagi, Bell and Obateru, 2024).

Counsellors and psychotherapists had to adapt to the new norm of having to work from home and many carried on seeing clients online or on the telephone. Therapists were more likely to self-disclose and clients were more likely to show concern for their therapists and ask how they were doing (Adams, 2024).

Therapy must have provided a lifeline to some clients who were struggling with the isolation or the opposite of being forced into close contact with family members with no respite. It also helped therapists cope because they had a purpose and something to focus on rather than the fear of what might happen.

The problem with the response to the pandemic was that it focused on physical health, but the strategy had a profound effect on psychological health. Since then, it has been found that there has been a legacy of disrupted education and lack of socialisation amongst children and young people (Duagi, Bell and Obateru, 2024).

Young people of school age have been found to have reduced resilience and personal agency as they lost the opportunity to be supported by staff in schools, including school counsellors, learning support workers and well-being leads. As young people came back to school, they felt fear and a lack of confidence and were less prepared for exams later, as for several years they were not required to do these (Crossman, 2022).

Crossman (2022) also talks about young people having less contact with the physical world and less in person social contact which has continued since COVID with the increased reliance on social media.

> In addition, spending so much time online produces a relatively narrow digest of news and information, resulting in young people often having constant exposure to potentially harmful influences, without the reprieve of something lighter. Stories, feeds, snaps and messages about distressing subjects, such as self-harm, intrusive thought and suicidal ideation, are consistently suggested or fed to them – sometimes with devastating effects.
>
> (Crossman, 2022)

The effects have been greater on those who already had mental health issues. The Centre for Mental Health report tells us that the most affected people have been younger people, racialised communities and those in the most deprived groups (Duagi, Bell and Obateru, 2024).

Since the pandemic many more people have sought help for their mental health and this has continued to grow, resulting in services being overwhelmed. The Report suggests that people are still living with the effects of Covid-19 times (Duagi, Bell and Obateru, 2024).

As a supervisor supporting counsellors working in different voluntary sector agencies and a tutor working with trainees, I have seen their cases become more complex and clients who would have been seen by statutory psychiatric or psychological services are now accessing counselling and are being seen by mainly volunteers or trainees in voluntary agencies. The demand on counsellors generally has increased and there is less recourse to statutory mental health services, whereas in the past if a person was seen too complex for a counsellor working in a charitable agency, there was a safety net and somewhere else to refer them to.

Working in an unsettled global environment: Wars and worldwide conflicts

Turbulent times are not a new thing, there have always been wars and conflicts between groups of people from early times in human history. What feels different now is the ease of access to information and the way the media can spike up our fears through speculation of worst-case scenarios. What is also different in the 20th century was the development of bombs/weapons which could cause mass destruction and lead to us feeling threatened with annihilation.

At the time of writing this we have had a Russian invasion into Ukraine and a continuing conflict there, a crisis in the Middle East with Israel and Palestine and other countries involved in fighting and killing of innocents and twelve ongoing civil wars in different parts of the world including Myanmar, Sudan, and Yemen.

See https://worldpopulationreview.com/country-rankings/countries-currently-at-war for more information.

What has this got to do with becoming a counsellor? World affairs are increasingly affecting our mental health and those of our potential clients. If we see reports of conflict on our screens including bombing, devastation and killings of innocent people on a daily basis, we are bound to feel gloomy and perhaps hopeless for the future of the world. The way conflicts are handled in the world by politicians of affluent countries and allies also affects our fears for the future: e.g., will the supplying of arms or interventions mean our safety might be jeopardised? Are we moving towards World War III?

Some therapists have been affected first hand because of their ethnic background, heritage and religion. The Israeli-Palestine conflict being a powerful example of this. This conflict is decades old, but became intensified on October 7, 2023 when Hamas, a Palestinian military group and political movement, invaded Israel killing at least 1,200 civilians and abducting 240 others, resulting in a massive retaliation of military attacks and a ground offensive by Israel on

Gaza and the displacement of people from this area plus other nations becoming involved. It is estimated that over 43,300 people have been killed as a result at the time of writing this (BBC News, 2024).

Sandi Mann, a Mental Health Practitioner was involved in a response to the surge of demand for counselling of Jewish people in her area. The attack on Israel retriggered previous trauma in Holocaust survivors and their descendants and journalists who witnessed the events. Jewish therapists were affected by the atrocities committed whilst needing to support their clients. She says people were coming for help to make things better but there was no way of taking the pain away (Mann, 2024).

Alaa Safi, (2024, p. 2) writes about her experience as a Palestinian counsellor living in the UK, working with refugees and asylum seekers. She says that having her family still living in Palestine with the ongoing war in Gaza 'has also brought me closer to their experiences and has provided me with a deeper understanding of the refugee experience and the experience of dehumanisation of refugees and other people in conflict zones.'

She goes on to say how her beliefs in humanity and morality have been shaken but her training and work in counselling and the support of colleagues and her community have helped her to keep going.

These are examples of how different therapists can be affected by worldwide events and those which affect their communities. Similarly, clients will bring in their anxieties and concerns and we may be able to meet them in our own anxiety. Adams (2024) says that it is a myth that we can leave our own stuff at the door of the therapy room.

> I am now convinced that this wonderful term 'bracketing' is simply an illusion, a comforting idea that bears no relation to reality [and] I am entirely human and I bring with me every single day into the therapy room a wealth of imperfections.
>
> (Adams, 2024, p. 3)

Circle of influence and control

Having looked at different worldwide and societal issues, we will now consider the idea of control and influence (Covey, 1989).

Worrying about matters we care deeply about which are beyond our control drains our energy. Things such as other people's reactions to us, unexpected events, the state of the economy or climate change as examples are outside of our control. We do have agency to control many things such as our interpretations of events, our thoughts and emotions or responses and decisions. You can control how you perceive things by challenging your own perspectives, you can control what you eat, how healthy you want to be, who you spend your time with and what you decide to read. We do also have the power to influence things, and this intersects what we directly can control with what is outside of our control. An example of this is when we change how we respond to others this may alter their reactions to us thus influencing others to change. Some of your discussions with clients may involve looking at what they have power to change and influence.

> ### Case study: Oliver
>
> Oliver spoke about feeling disturbed by worldwide events and emotionally impacted particularly after learning about the historical genocide in Cambodia. His humanitarian values urged him to take action but what could he do? He felt powerless and drained. He described himself as sensitive and had begun researching into the impacts on the country. This was affecting his sleep and intruding on his daily thoughts. The therapist noticed he was hyper-focusing on this and it was affecting his wellbeing. He introduced Oliver to the theory of circle of influence and control. Oliver identified what he was in control of such as how much time he spent reading about this, being selective about what he read, making choices about volunteering and travel. He decided to make use of the opportunity at University to go abroad and to make a documentary about the devastating effects on the people. His goal shifted to make use of his agency: He could raise awareness but not change what had happened. This channelled his energies to make use of his values of being a caring, kind person.

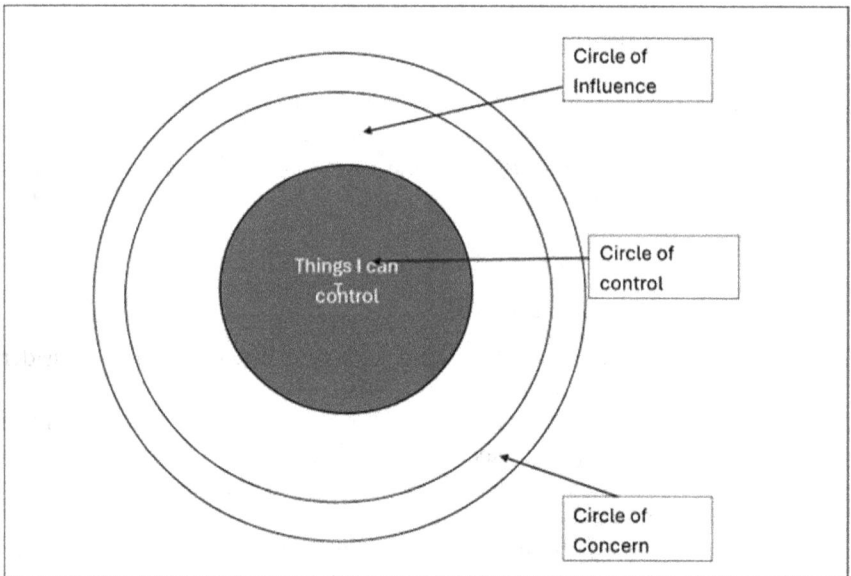

Diagram Circle of Influence and Control

Figure 12.2 Circle of influence and control

List the things you are concerned about in the world in the outer circle. There is little point in spending our lives in this domain as we literally have no agency here. Living our lives worrying about this circle situates us in a powerless position of frustration and angst. Consider what actually is within your control, next consider what you may influence remembering you can take charge of your own efforts here but not the actual outcome of your efforts. Remember we are not in control of the outcomes here, but this has the potential to effect change.

So, with the issues looked at in this chapter like climate change, some examples of action may be to make small changes to your life to become greener or join an organisation which campaigns for action (e.g., Greenpeace, Friends of the Earth etc.) or in terms of the worldwide political situation you may join peace marches or write to your MP regarding international policies and aid.

Ponder points

How much of your time do you spend worrying about things outside of your control?
What was it like to focus your energy on what is within your power?
How do you think you will work with your clients using this model of influence and control?

Conclusion

It is impossible to keep the world out of the counselling room. Psychological assessments and diagnoses of an individual do not consider the person in context and this chapter hopes to challenge any assumptions about therapy as an individual practice. Our society forms us and is part of us. We have seen how structural oppression plays a large part in the development of mental health problems and how disadvantaged people are affected more by worldwide issues.

We have encouraged you to become more conversant with important current issues so as to avoid denial and complacency. Also, we have examined contemporary trends in social media, recognising the powerful influence of the online world. As therapists and clients, we are impacted by events in the world and experience the anxiety of difficult and challenging times. Consequently, it is important to address our own feelings and issues that feel out of our control.

A key factor has been this 'anxiety' and recognising that it is normal and acceptable given the challenges and difficulties the world is facing. Rather than worrying about things that are outside of our control, we can look at what we can influence and take action in line with our values and beliefs. We may then be able to support others to do the same.

This chapter has moved us to more of a 'we' position rather than an 'us and them' stance. We are all part of the world and need to be alongside our clients in their suffering.

References

Adams, M. (2024) *The Myth of the Untroubled Therapist*. London: Routledge.

Aspey, L. (2021) The big issue: Breaking out of the climate bubble. *Therapy Today*, 32(9). Available from www.bacp.co.uk/bacp-journals/therapy-today/2021/november-2021/the-bigissue/ [date accessed 2 December 2024].

BACP (2021) The Big Interview: Nick Totton. Available from www.bacp.co.uk/bacp-journals/therapy-today/2021/november/the-big-interview/ [date accessed 16 December, 2024].

BBC News (2024) Nearly 70% of Gaza war dead verified by UN are women and children. Available from www.bbc.co.uk/news/articles/cn5well1pgdo?oref=d_brief_nl [date accessed 13 December, 2024].

BBC News (2025) What is Hamas and why is it fighting with Israel in Gaza? Available from www.bbc.co.uk/news/world-middle-east-67039975?0=utm_source=ground.news [date accessed 3 January, 2025].

Campbell, W., Tamasese, K., and Waldergrave, C. (2001) *Just Therapy Family Therapy: Exploring the Field's Past, Present and Possible Futures*. Dulwich Centre Publications.

Covey, S. (1989) *The 7 Habits of Highly Effective People*. New York: Simon & Schuster.

Crossman, F. (2022, December) The legacy of Covid-19: Every little bit helps. *BACP Children, Young People and Families Journal*. Available from www.bacp.co.uk/bacp-journals/bacp-children-young-people-and-families-journal/december-2022/the-legacy-of-covid-19/ [date accessed 8 December, 2024].

Duagi, D., Bell, A., and Obateru, A. (2024) Covid-19 and the Nation's Mental Health: A review of the evidence published so far. Centre for Mental Health. Available from www.centreformentalhealth.org.uk/publications/covid-19-and-the-nations-mental-health/ [date accessed 20 November, 2024].

Erikson, E. H. (1950) *Childhood and Society*. London: Vintage Books.

Hickman, C., Marks, E., and Pihkala, P. (2021) Climate anxiety in children and young people and their beliefs about government responses to climate change: A global survey. *Lancet Planet Health*, 5(12), 863–873.

International Crisis Group (2024) 10 conflicts to watch in 2024. Available from www.crisisgroup.org/global/10-conflicts-watch-2024 [date accessed 3, January 2025].

Jackson, C. (2020) Facing the reality of climate change. *Therapy Today*, 31(2), 18–21.

Johnston, W. M. and Davey, G. C. (1997) The psychological impact of negative TV news bulletins: The catastrophizing of personal worries. *British Journal Psychology*, 88(1), 85–91.

Lee, C. C. and Humphrey, M. (2023) Advocacy and working with individual clients beyond traditional therapy models. In Winter, L. A. and Charura, D. (Eds), *The Handbook of Social Justice in Psychological Therapies Power, Politics, Change*. London: SAGE Publications.

Licoppe, C. (2004) Connected presence: The emergence of a new repertoire for managing social relationships in a changing communication technoscape. *Environment and Planning D: Society and Space*, 22(1), 135–156.

Mann, S. (2024) A community in traumatic stress: Workplace matters. Available from www.bacp.co.uk/news/news-from-bacp/blogs/2024/blogs-and-vlogs-2024/4-january-a -community-in-traumatic-stress/Date [date accessed 7 January, 2025].

Pihkala, P. (2019) *Climate Anxiety*. Helsinki: MIELA Mental Health Finland.

Popat, A. and Tarrant, C. (2023) Exploring adolescents' perspectives on social media and mental health and well-being: A qualitative literature review, *Clinical Child Psychology and Psychiatry*, 28(1), 323–337.

Reese, R. F., Swank, J. M., and Sturm, D. C. (2023) A national survey of helping professionals on climate change and counselling. *American Counseling Association: Journal of Humanistic Counseling*, 62, 201–215.

Scott, C. F., Marcu, G., Anderson, R. E., Newman, M. W., and Schoenebeck, S. (2023, April). Trauma-informed social media: Towards solutions for reducing and healing online harm. *Proceedings of the 2023 CHI Conference on Human Factors in Computing Systems*, 1–20.

Safi, A. (2024) My practice. *Therapy Today*, 35(3), 44.

Seth, A., Maxwell, J., Dey, C., Le Feuvre, C., and Patrick, R. (2023) Understanding and managing psychological distress due to climate change. *Australian Journal of General Practice*, 52(5), 263–268.

Silva, J. F. B. and Coburn, J. (2023) Therapists' experience of climate change: A dialectic between personal and professional. *CPR*, 23, 417–431.

Walker, C., Johnson, K., and Cunningham, L. (2012) *Community Psychology and the Socio-economics of Mental Distress: International Perspectives*. Basingstoke: Palgrave Macmillan.

World Population Review (2024) Counties currently at war 2024. Available from https:// worldpopulationreview.com/country-rankings/countries-currently-at-war [date accessed 13 December, 2024].

Chapter 13

Self-care

Boundaries not bubble bath!

Tara Fox

Introduction

This chapter helps you to consider self-kindness, self-compassion and community, thus reframing self-care as a compassionate activity essential for working in the service of others. Awareness of healthy boundaries and the influence of intergenerational beliefs on care for self are discussed prompting you to consider the historical influences of your family.

Research with trainee therapists shows ways to restore and replenish the self. Reframing self-care as an interconnected and interdependent activity is explored, as doing this alone can be difficult and it can be achieved with the support of others

Finally, this chapter emphasises that to be there for others, we need to have self-compassion and then attend to ours needs.

In particular, this chapter will look at:

- attending to self
- our support network
- intergenerational influences
- healthy boundaries
- self-compassion
- a personal response to caring for self
- self-care as community care
- trainee therapist self-care plans.

Attending to self

I remember reading a student journal summary in which the writer pleaded for help and advice about this mysterious self-care that tutors expected her to know how to do. The student fed back how tutors had casually mentioned in class how people should take care of themselves during the teaching sessions, assuming that people knew how to do this. She shouted through her words as I read them on the page – 'How can I do this when I do not know how? How

DOI: 10.4324/9781003405757-14

can I be expected to do this without being taught how?' I gave her written feedback and guidance along with an apology. This apology felt important because the teaching team expected students to know and had not covered the topic enough in the curriculum.

Since then, I have placed more attention on the holistic self of the counselling trainee including their learner and practitioner dimensions, taking students through psychoeducation, resilience training, mindful awareness, and the development of self-compassion.

Attending to the whole self of the trainee in education may seem surprising until we consider how burnout, compassion fatigue, and vicarious trauma are possibilities for front-line work in the healthcare professions.

The term burnout was originally defined by Maslach and Jackson (1981) as a syndrome of exhaustion and depersonalisation, a state of loss of feeling and sense of being detached from oneself that impacts negatively on professional achievement especially affecting employees working with others, e.g., in social work, health care, and teaching (Frieiro Padín et al., 2021).

Compassion fatigue is a term originally described by Figley (1995) to be the emotional exhaustion of caring for patients. You may wonder how this could apply to counselling when listening to other people's stories about their lives.

Ponder point

What harm can there be when 'listening' to others?

When we feel supported by the place we work in, when we are not overloaded by demands for our time and pressures to meet the expectations of others, and when engaged in activities that bring us joy then we may feel robust and grounded to listen to other people's lives in such a way that we are not affected emotionally ourselves. However, when we are out of touch with ourselves, we may not notice we need something and can keep on taking on more and more, adding to our workload and becoming weakened through the process. Without proper barriers to protect ourselves from other people's distress then we can become overloaded. This can lead to detaching oneself as a form of coping or feeling numb and unable to adapt to the intensity of the demands. This can feel very frightening for people.

Attending to the self is the first step in self-care and links with the principle of self-respect whereby practitioners have an ethical responsibility to foster one's own self-knowledge, integrity and care for self (BACP, 2018). This involves awareness of self, a coming out of the automatic pilot mode to a fuller sense of the present moment. Being in autopilot mode has its advantages providing us with efficient ways to achieve tasks but it brings problems too. Have you ever travelled home and wondered how you got there? This is an example of being in this state. The more we live in this state the less we are aware of our own needs and therefore we can become task-focused, a human doing rather than a human being. Being task focused takes us away from being in relationship with others as we are not concentrating on being with a person in a genuine way.

In some health care roles, the person is doing something to someone such as practical care or taking bloods which the Austrian philosopher and educator Martin Buber called an 'I–It' relationship (see Buber, 2008).

In counselling the role requires a 'use of self' something described by Buber to be an 'I–thou' relationship of holistic care. This distinction is significant as one describes the other as an object, the other as 'kin' in recognition of the connection between client and counsellor in a relational interaction where one mutually influences the other.

The following exercise is a practical strategy for attending to yourself and one you can use any time of the day to reconnect with being you rather than doing tasks.

Exercise in attending to self

Sitting or standing in an upright position with eyes lowered or closed begin to sense how you are feeling in this moment. See if you can accept whatever is there without judging this.

Shift your attention to your breath, breathing in and breathing out. This is a body that is already breathing, and you are just joining in with it.

Thoughts come into your mind like thoughts will always do. Accept these are there and return to your breath noticing the feeling of the breath as it enters and leaves the body.

Gently begin to bring some movement into your body such as tilting your head from side to side or moving your shoulders. Thank yourself for giving you this time. Say in your mind I do this for me I do this for others.

What did you notice from doing this brief exercise? Maybe you realised how tired you are, how you have been putting something off, how peaceful you felt. Whatever you realised this is helpful information for you to consider.

What do you need to do for yourself next? You may need to address a worry or confront something you have been putting off, ask someone for help, maybe you need to get more regular sleep.

Begin to practice this short exercise throughout the day to break up the parts of the day into moments. You could begin to do this when waiting for the train, bus, kettle to boil, waiting for the lift etc. Bringing yourself back to you throughout the day can help you to gain distance between your thoughts and yourself. It can help you to slow down and notice more which can help you to make better choices about what you say and do.

I do not have time to sit down

It's amazing how much time we have but we tend to fill it with things that are our priorities. There are 168 hours in a week. Consider where the pockets of time are for you to slow down a little as the example below shows:

> In my administration role, I feel a lot of satisfaction from achieving the tasks set out for the day, but I often feel like the days are the same. I have been trying to be more in the moment, which has helped me feel less stressed at work. Little changes like waiting at the copier for the work to be done and taking a few mindful breaths means I can notice more of what I need. I give myself time to take 5 min breaks drinking my coffee and enjoying this rather than slurping it on my desk while doing other tasks. It sounds simple and I can't believe I never thought of this before.

Worrying about the future does nothing to take care of it. John Kabat-Zinn, founder of the mindfulness stress-based reduction (MBSR) course reminds us how we take care of the future if we take care of now. (Kabat-Zinn, 2004). In other words, bring more of our awareness to the present moment by taking notice of this moment in time, grounding ourselves by noticing how our feet feel in our shoes or on the ground, and the feeling of our breath entering and leaving the body.

Mindful awareness is linked to emotional regulation and locus of control (Guendelman, Medeiros and Rampes, 2017). Basically, this means the more aware you are of the present moment the calmer you are, and therefore more able to make better choices about what to do. It is as if a little gap unfolds between your inner reaction and outer responses aided by more of a helicopter view of what is going on in that moment.

Try pockets of mindful awareness throughout the day. A few minutes here and there make a big difference to your ability to do this. A further area to review when considering caring for yourself is your support network which is often skewed towards supporting others rather than oneself.

Our support network

When you begin counselling training, you are considering working in the field of mental health. This is humbling and rewarding because we are in a position of helping others, being of service to others, and giving our time and attention to a fellow human being who is suffering in some way. Knowing you can make a difference is rewarding and the ripple effects of counselling we can only guess at, but it is likely to affect many others who have also been struggling to see their loved ones in emotional pain. We also need to make some changes in our lives to accommodate more self-care so that we can do this work.

Activity

Support network at work

- In your current role who do you experience as supportive of your work?

Support network at home and in your community

- Now consider who you experience as supportive outside of work.
- Reviewing this experience, what do you notice? Is there anything that needs to change?
- Do you need to develop your support network?

Seeing who is in your support network can be a challenging experience especially if the people you have named take more from you than you receive from them. In some cases, you may find it hard to name people and if this applies to you then perhaps you are not reaching out for support. Being resilient is not about being self-sufficient but about asking for help when you are struggling and knowing it is OK to do this. See Chapter 10 for a discussion on trainee therapist resilience along with other barriers to development. Often our approach to helping ourselves has in part been inherited from our families, passed down to us through stories and modelled to us through our parents and family elders.

Intergenerational influences

The families and communities we grow up in influence our attitudes to caring for ourselves as well as others. They also react to the changes we may make in this area, sometimes trying to pull us back into the usual ways of behaving. At times this can be hard to navigate and pulls on our conscience when we try to create the space needed to care for ourselves. One way of understanding the reactions of others can be interpreted through the work of John Byng-Hall (1985), a systemic psychotherapist who made use of the language of the theatre to make sense of relational dynamics. He reminds us how family scenes or dramas are part and parcel of family life.

Family scripts according to Byng-Hall are the expected behaviours based on the family's belief system. The script enables everyone to predict behaviours and is followed often without question. An example of a mini script is how the family deals with emotions. Feeling unable to cope or being seen as vulnerable may be judged to be unacceptable and the family script may present as 'just get on with it' or 'that's life.' Self-care is one area where scripts can conspire against us and is a larger pattern of how the family treats time for themselves.

The following case study shows how intergenerational influences impact on our ability to care for ourselves and how we can see this more objectively through the lens of family scripts pulling and pushing us to be the same as we were.

Case study: Sam

In my family growing up we all understood how we should make the most of each day by achieving and working through the tasks we knew we had to do. Home-work before playing, chores before resting, not being selfish and we all knew that we had to meet mum and dad's expectations or else there would be a big argu-ment. I remember my older brother once ran off instead of putting the shopping away and my dad chased him down the street and told him he should be grateful for having food in the house and the least he could do was to help pack it away. It was pretty strict in that sense. I had to help mum look after my younger siblings, and we were all taught that we should work hard and then we would be rewarded for our efforts.

When I got older, I fell into the role of carer for my wider family and enjoyed helping as I did not mind. I felt a sense of purpose and achievement from being there for people. My mum was the same, helping my aunties and grandparents when they needed it.

Basically, you could say we had a family script of being there for others and not making a fuss.

When I started counselling training, I found it hard to fit in time for my studies and started to feel stressed. I didn't want to let my family down and felt under pressure to carry on rushing about fitting in extra jobs people needed me to do. I got behind with my work and for the first time had to say no to picking up my sister's son from nursery. She got really angry and told me I was being selfish. I burst into tears and spoke to my course tutor. She explained how people were not used to me considering what I needed and were finding this difficult as my behaviour was impacting them. I was encouraged to set boundaries with the help I was giving so I could set time aside for myself. This filled me with dread, and I began therapy to work this all through.

The inherited family beliefs around caring for self or others can feel like a strict rule for how to live our lives. It can feel isolating to question the way things are when other family members do not see your point of view. It helps when we consider the origin of such family beliefs and consequent scripts around how our families 'do' emotions, care for themselves, or care for others. Recognising the patterns that have been passed on to us can help us to have compassion for the resistance within our families who hold dearly onto these rules and attempt to restore stability by pulling us back into line.

Activity

- What patterns can you recognize that have been passed down in your family history?
- What are the family scripts around emotions and self-care in your family or origin?
- Who is allowed to 'do' which emotions and how?
- What are the scripts around caring for self?

Within the metaphor of theatre, scripts can be rewritten and in that sense are what Byng Hall called 'improvised scripts' i.e., new ways of relating that let go of some of the intergenerational ones. It may be that in considering self-care you are indeed improvising and paving a new way forward for the next generations in your family. This requires you to give yourself permission to change, a theme that was found in a research study by Daldorph and Hill (2022) investigating the perceived impact of counselling training on students' personal relationships.

As you gain new perspectives and experiment with new ways of relating this is inevitably going to impact on others and your relationship with yourself. One helpful way to consider how to practically implement these changes is to hold stronger boundaries.

Healthy boundaries

When students brainstorm ways of caring for themselves the bath idea often crops up as a reliable option but unless we can set boundaries for ourselves, baths will not help alone. I remember a student who was also a radiographer telling me she was having four baths a day to manage her stress, but it was not working. Her family script was to work harder when things became stressful and not to give up. Being stressed and off sick went against her family's beliefs, and she was fearful of being judged as a failure. The student group challenged her beliefs that were passed down from the family and encouraged her to make a stand at work by taking the time off she needed to recover from workplace stress. Although this felt hard for her to do, with the support from the group she felt better equipped to stand up for her rights as an employee and as a daughter who was suffering.

This example is extreme but is a typical boundary violation of the self. We weaken our emotional boundaries by denying our true selves for example:

- Pretending to agree with others' opinions
- Going along with an idea/activity you don't really want to do
- Using drugs, alcohol, nicotine, caffeine and sugars to avoid being with yourself

- Not resting when you feel tired
- Pushing yourself to do too much, for example, too much exercise, too much work, too much cleaning.

Our historical influences when growing up may include numerous examples of unhealthy boundary setting, for example, being told to go to school when you are poorly. These micro experiences impact on our understanding of ourselves, making us consider other people's needs before our own and influence our capacity to set healthy boundaries. Something which Rogers (1959) called our conditions of worth.

Activity

Think about how you may weaken your emotional boundaries, for example saying yes when everything inside you is shouting no!

- How do you feel inside? Where do you hold this in your body?
- Bring your hand to that part of your body and reassure your felt sense that it is OK to say no when you mean no.
- Give thanks to yourself for trying to protect yourself by agreeing when you mean no. It makes sense that you would want to keep yourself safe.
- In your mind or out loud now say 'no' three times.
- Notice how this feels different.... Where do you feel this sensation in your body? An openness, a strength, and powerfulness perhaps?
- Remember there is always a part of you who knows the boundary of no. It just needs some encouragement to come out.
- What did you discover about yourself through doing this activity?

Setting boundaries can be learned through practice. Practice saying no in everyday life instead of 'sorry no.' I had to stick a note on the fridge to remind me: 'What do I want?' *Not* 'what can I give?' Although thinking of others first is my default position, I am more able to notice my tendency to want to give and therefore allow myself time to adapt to a mindset of: 'What is reasonable to offer given my current circumstances?'

This perspective has developed over my lifetime through the consideration of self-compassion. Without self-compassion it is doubtful we will notice we need anything at all, nor will we be able to give ourselves the necessary permission to take some of the time available and bracket this off for self-care.

Self-compassion

Kristen Neff and research colleagues (2011), who study self-compassion, remind us how there is a big difference between self-esteem and self-compassion. The definition of self-esteem is a global evaluation of self-worth according to Neff and she points out that increasing self-esteem is not necessarily the way forward if we want to motivate ourselves. Our personal self-criticism impacts negatively on our self-esteem and no matter how much you beat yourself up this will not motivate you to do better because you are putting yourself under threat. You may think that you need to develop your self-esteem particularly if you have experienced a lot of criticism in your life, but the following table outlines some enlightening differences summarised and adapted from the work of Neff et al. (2011):

Self-esteem	Self-compassion
Judging ourselves as better or worse than others	Nonjudgmental and self-kindness
Being above average	Accepting our flaws
A global evaluation of self-worth	Common humanity – how we are similar
Asks am I a good person or a bad person	Empathy for oneself as imperfect beings
Feeling special	Feeling supportive of oneself
Put other people down to make oneself feel better	Wanting health and well-being for yourself
Requires success for the standards we set	Noticing when we are suffering and accepting, we have done what we can

Looking at this we can see self-esteem looks outwards and compares to others whereas self-compassion looks inwards to support and accept ourselves.

Studies by Neff and McGeehee (2010) and Neff, Hsieh, and Dejitthirat (2005) remind us how we are responsive to warmth, comforting tones of voice, and compassion. This is more of a motivator than self-criticism and many studies show how self-compassion is associated with strong mental health and a feeling of self-worth (MacBeth and Gumley, 2012).

Our parents' attitudes towards the need for self-compassion impact our capacity to do this. Typically, this means a reconsideration of the conditioning we have gone through to adulthood.

A study in Australia with foster carers regarding self-care (Miko, Berger, and Krishnamoorthy 2023) highlights barriers to caring for oneself including the need for a culture to positively promote and regard personal wellbeing. Participants in their study explained obstacles such as guilt, selfishness, and incompetence arising from internalised stigma. They needed a self-care plan to keep them on track with attending to their own well-being. Similarly, in counselling and psychotherapy training educators place value on the need to prioritise caring for oneself, but individuals also need to increase self-awareness to know what they need and recognise the times that signal more self-care is needed.

Working in the field of mental health is a caring profession and yet the demands of the system are largely at odds with the message of prioritising self-care. The organisational pressures and client demands may generate conflicts with attending to self. However, if we reframe caring for oneself as central to being of service to others then there is a rational need for this care that legitimises and gives permission to pace oneself.

A personal response to caring for self

When I feel compassion for myself, I notice how hard things are for me and how I need to put aside some time for myself. Being more present with myself I notice I am tired, I see I am struggling to concentrate and I take a break. If I am in the automatic pilot mode of achieving tasks, I can make many quick wins such as ticking off emails or making phone calls. This is when I am working in the urgent and important areas of my daily life. I enjoy the times I am arranging a meeting, planning an event for the future, scheduling some time for writing or blocking out time for other things. This is where I am focusing on the important but not urgent parts of my life. Those aspects are for my personal growth but there are still times when this is not possible and self-compassion is needed for this too.

We may feel from time to time that our self-care practices are working well for us and at other times they may work against us because they no longer fit in with our schedules and work patterns.

Not keeping up with any self-care plan could feed into more guilt and lack of care. Caring for oneself might include being OK with going off sick, saying no to extra work, not squeezing in a new client or responsibility into a busy schedule or changing one's mind about an activity that has already been agreed. The work of Gael Lindenfeld (1986) inspired me during my initial professional therapy training, providing me with a list of assertive rights.

In particular, I found two that I needed to learn: *I have the right to say no and the right to change my mind.* These rights empowered me to work on my family scripts of women who care, are accommodating, need to help others, and not let anyone else down.

Self-care as community care

The work of Shelley Tygielski, a self-care coach, meditation teacher, and social justice champion speaks about self-care as community care widening the notion of 'self' to include family, community, nature, and all living beings (Tygielski, 2021). Widening our focus from oneself to others reframes self-care as more of a community activity, reducing isolation and guilt typically felt when considering our needs. She explains guilt can be countered by knowing we are not alone and by setting up small communities of support to make each other accountable for wellness.

Activity

Think about the different groups you belong to. Work teams, parenting groups, community/sport/faith/charity groups. Human connection matters. We are interdependent.

Who could help you in return for any help you can offer?

Agree to check in with each other about your wellness – ask 'are you pacing yourself?'

In your course group, you can offer help and receive self-care through sharing resources such as books, recommending helpful podcasts, setting up peer support groups for essay writing, or creative ways to work with clients.

Make a realistic self-care plan to serve you well and keep it simple. See this as a living document that needs reviewing regularly to check if it's still working out for you in your community of self-care. Teaming up with others can help.

What do trainee therapists have in their self-care plans?

I organised a conference on spirituality and creativity with 53 trainee therapists in attendance discussing together in a world cafe style of participation (Brown and Isaacs, 2005) the self-care practices needed for working with clients 'soul to soul.'

Students wrote down their ideas on flip paper and sticky notes moving around tables in a café ambience environment. After analysing the ideas and grouping them into families we can see how at the root of the issue we need grounding and boundaries as a foundation. The trunk of the tree shows how connecting back to the self to know our limits requires giving oneself time and space alone to contemplate. Self-compassion is also needed to acknowledge how we feel, and bodily movement serves as a connective tissue to the self. This then channels our energy through two main branches of creativity and self-soothing leading to the many fruits of the tree shown here as leaves. Perhaps this could be a useful starting point for your own self-care plan.

Ponder points

Looking at all of their responses what stands out for you?

What would you like to pick from the tree of ideas?

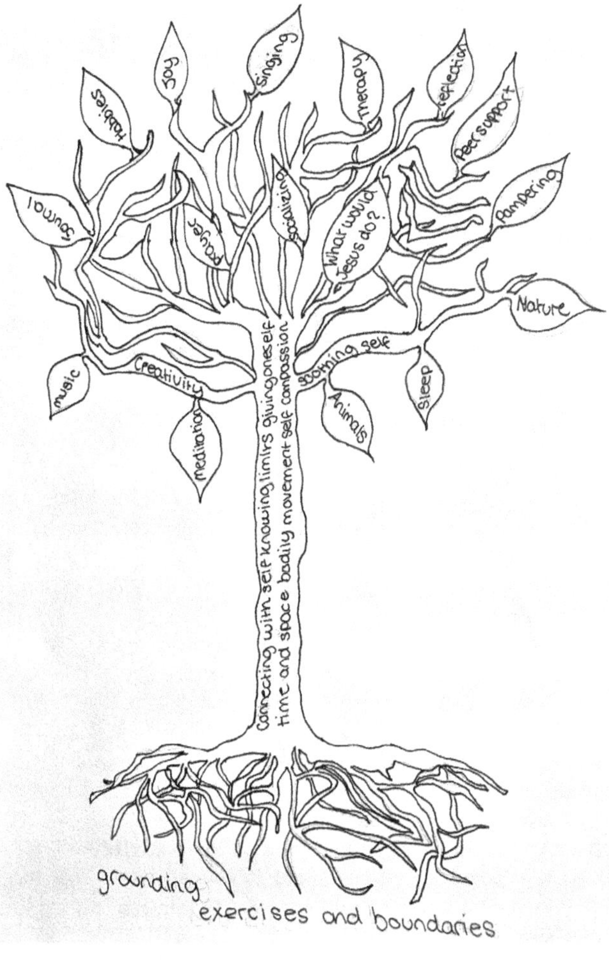

Figure 13.1 Tree of self-care findings

Conclusion

This chapter has taken the reader through a fresh look at self-care considering the need for self-compassion to notice the necessity to attend to yourself, how our support network is so important, and how the generations before us influence our attitude to self-care. It has also raised the need for healthy boundaries and self-kindness. Self-care is really an interconnected and interdependent activity. We all need to be nourished and rely on others to flourish in the world.

References

Barton, H. (2019) An exploration of the experiences that counsellors have of taking care of their own mental, emotional and spiritual well-being. *Counselling and Psychotherapy Research*, 20(3), 516–524.

Byng-Hall, J. (1985) The family script: a useful bridge between theory and practice. *Journal of Family Therapy*, 7(3), 301–305.

Brown, J., and Isaacs, D. (2005) *The World Cafe: Shaping our futures ' through conversations that matter.* Berrett-Koehler Publishers.

Buber, M. (2008) *I and Thou:100ᵗʰ Anniversary Reissue.* London: Simon & Schuster.

Daldorph, A. and Hill, S. (2022) The perceived impact of counselling training on students' personal relationships. *Counselling & Psychotherapy Research*, October, 1.

Figley, C. R. (Ed.) (1995) *Compassion Fatigue: Coping with Secondary Traumatic Stress Disorder in Those Who Treat the Traumatised.* New York: Routledge.

Frieiro, P., Carmen, V.-D., Fernandez, T., and Gonzalez-Rodriguez, R. (2021) Burnout in health social work: An international systematic review (2000–2020). *European Journal of Social Work*, 24(6), 1051–1065.

Guendelman, S., Medeiros, S., and Rampes, H. (2017) Mindfulness and emotion regulation: Insights from neurobiological, psychological, and clinical studies, *Frontiers in Psychology*, 8.

Kabat-Zinn, J. (2004) *Wherever You go There You Are: Mindfulness for everyday life.* London: Piaktus Books.

Lindenfeld, G. (1986) *Assert Yourself.* London: Thorsons Press.

MacBeth, A., and Gumley, A. (2012) Exploring compassion: A meta-analysis of the association between self-compassion and psychopathology. *Clinical Psychology Review*, 32(6), 545–552.

Maslach, C. and Jackson, S. E. (1981). *Maslach Burnout Inventory Manual* (with a special supplement 'Burnout in Education' by Richard L. Schwab). Palo Alto, California: Consulting Psychologists Press.

Miko, A. L., Berger, E., and Krishnamoorthy, G. (2023) Exploring self-care practices in foster carers: A qualitative study. *Journal of Public Child Welfare*, 17(2), 333–355.

Miller, J. J. (2017) Self-care among healthcare social workers: An exploratory study. *Social Work in Health Care*, 56(10), 865–883.

Neff, K. (2003) Self-compassion: An alternative conceptualization of a healthy attitude toward oneself. *Self and Identity*, 2(2), 85–101.

Neff, K. D. (2011) Self-compassion, self-esteem, and well-being. *Social and Personality Psychology Compass*, 5(1), 1–12.

Neff, K. D., and McGeehee, P. (2010) Self-compassion and psychological resilience among adolescents and young adults. *Self and Identity*, 9, 225–240.

Neff, K. D., Hsieh, Y., and Dejitterat, K. (2005) Self-compassion, achievement goals, and coping with academic failure. *Self and Identity*, 4(3), 263–287.

Rogers, C. (1959) A theory of therapy, personality, and interpersonal relationships, as developed in the client-centered framework. In Koch, S. (Ed.), *Psychology: A Study of a Science, Vol. 3: Formulations of the Person and the Social Context.* New York: McGraw-Hill.

Tygielski, S (2021) *Sit Down to Rise Up: How Radical Self-Care Can Change the World.* Novato, CA: New World Library.

Chapter 14

Super Vision

Embracing the opportunity

Jayne Godward

Introduction

When I first went for my supervision, I wasn't prepared for this and did not know what to expect. My supervisor was provided by the agency where I had just started placement and seemed a friendly, non-judgemental person but I didn't know what to talk about when I arrived, and I expect she had to lead the first few sessions.

Your training may prepare you for supervision and you may have engaged with peer supervision on your course, however you may still be unsure how to spend this time with your new supervisor.

Personally, I think that you will appreciate its value, the more supervision you have and the more you get into the thick of your counselling practice.

The aim of this chapter is to help you to begin to understand what clinical supervision is and its potential, as well as understand why it is required. Hopefully it will enable you to make the most out of this opportunity.

It will look at:

- what supervision is
- the functions of supervision
- choosing a supervisor
- preparing for supervision
- bringing client cases to supervision
- the importance of feedback
- requirements for supervision.

What is supervision?

Often trainees confuse clinical supervision with management supervision which they may have had as part of their professional work as social workers or nurses etc.

In managerial supervision there is an element of monitoring your competency and effectiveness and this may take place within your workplace with a senior

DOI: 10.4324/9781003405757-15

manager or team leader to whom you wouldn't want to appear incompetent or unsure of what you are doing. Whereas, although clinical supervisors do have a monitoring function in that they have to make sure that you are abiding by legal and ethical practice, this will be done in a more discursive and collaborative style usually encouraging you to look at the situation and what is involved rather than them being judgemental and authoritarian. You will be with a more experienced person who is primarily there to support you in your development rather than appraising your performance.

They will be aiming to help you reflect on and review your work and will usually expect you to lead the supervisory session and will help you to identify your individual training and development needs.

The following table highlights some of the main differences between clinical and managerial supervision, however a lot of this will depend on the individual supervisor and the organisation where the supervision is taking place.

Clinical supervision	Managerial supervision
Person is a qualified practitioner with more experience than the supervisee not usually a line manager	Supervisor is a senior person in your organisation or a line manager
Supervisor monitors legal and ethical practice but will do this in a collaborative/ discursive way where possible	Manager will monitor competence and effectiveness and assesses performance may encourage discussion but has more authority
The supervisee will normally set the agenda and bring client work or issues which they choose	Often there will be an agenda set by the manager or their organisation – less supervisee led.
Main role is to help you reflect and review your work with your clients to ensure best practice	Main role is to ensure effective practice and may be goal or target driven by the aims of the organisation

The following case study helps to show how managerial and clinical supervision have different functions.

Case study

Angie was an ex-social worker who had just started therapeutic counselling training. She was working with her new supervisor. She was discussing her concern about a client, Siobhan, who was in an abusive relationship where her partner constantly undermined her and sometimes hit her, but she had no intention of leaving her as she was frightened of being alone.

Angie wanted to step in and advise her client. She wanted to report her to the police and take action on her behalf. In her social work role, she would have done this and it would have been expected of her by her managerial supervisor.

> Her clinical supervisor helped her to look at the ethical and legal aspects to this case. Firstly, the social worker's role is very different and secondly Siobhan was not a vulnerable adult but a deputy head teacher in a local school. If any action was to be taken, she needed to decide on this (her autonomy).
>
> Angie needed to stay in her client's frame of reference and help Siobhan explore her situation and look at what she wanted for her well-being (beneficence).
>
> Her supervisor challenged her to revisit the ethical principles she had studied on her course and to look at where the safeguarding aspects of the law applied or not.

Here it can be seen that supervision is the place to explore how to work with clients, to think about what we should be doing and to look at our motives for certain actions or proposed interventions. A tendency I see in new trainees is a wish to fix or solve the client's problems without staying with or being with the client. Here Angie did not have the same responsibility and duty of care that she had as a social worker with her clients and her supervisor had to help her understand her new role and how she needed to work with the client. There was an element of challenge in the session but space for Angie to look at how she felt about the situation and to express her concerns.

The functions of supervision

Generally, there are three main functions of supervision including the normative, formative and restorative functions which have been written about at length by Inskipp and Proctor (2009).

The *normative* function was exemplified in the Angie Case Study as her supervisor helped her look at the norms of counselling practice and what was expected of her in terms of legal and ethical aspects.

Hawkins and Smith (2012, p. 63) label this the qualitative function in which it is likened to quality control. During your training your supervisor carries some responsibility for your work and is ensuring that you maintain a certain standard and is likely to challenge any unethical or legal practice.

The *formative* function is about development. Your supervisor is there to support you with this process of becoming a counsellor and will be with you as you take the steps to becoming a practitioner. Part of the supervisory role is to educate and to meet your developmental needs. This may take the form of your supervisor sharing their experiences, helping you understand your counselling model or clients' issues or giving you information or just helping you identify your learning needs more.

The formative function is more important for you in training as you can gain knowledge from this experienced practitioner and learn from them. Later in your career this function may be less important.

For example, I was recently discussing what it means to be a person-centred counsellor and what our work is about. I was challenging my supervisee about the idea of light bulb moments as they seemed to think that was the aim of counselling rather than providing a space for someone to explore and slowly reach conclusions about themselves. We also looked at hidden agendas which therapists might have even when they are supposed to be unconditional. Some formative supervision may be more like teaching but often this is more subtle and more interactive.

Finally, the *restorative* function is an important function as it is about your well-being as a trainee therapist in relation to your client work. This is not to be confused with personal therapy which focusses purely on your personal issues although there often feels to be an overlap here.

Many supervisors start their sessions by checking in with their supervisees and asking how they are. This is not just a polite thing to do, it is an essential part of supervision as we are keeping an eye on the well-being of our supervisees and also making sure they are fit to practice or at least are looking after themselves.

Self-respect is the bottom line. If we don't look after ourselves as counsellors, we can't attend to the needs of others. We have explored this more in Chapter 13 where we look at self-care. Your supervision is a good place to look at how you are doing and how your life is intersecting with your professional practice. Supervision can be refreshing as it is a chance to off load and explore what is going on and share the strains of working with certain clients.

It cannot be stressed enough how we can be adversely affected by empathising and working with clients who are in distress or crisis and our supervision is a way of coping with this. But your supervisor is also paying attention to unhealthy working environments which we may find ourselves in both as students and qualified counsellors. Sometimes, the only way to protect your well-being is to step out of this.

Occasionally, it isn't the actual placement that is unhealthy, it is the type of work we have chosen which is too taxing for us personally. My own example is when I was drawn to working in cancer support counselling due to my own history of having a parent with cancer. What I didn't realise was that I was putting my hand into the fire by doing this. I worked at the service for nearly a year but started to realise that I was losing empathy for my clients and was starting to see life in a very bleak way.

My supervisor helped me explore what was going on and I realised that the work was wearing me down and I was being triggered by memories from my past. I came to realise through supervision that I had been drawn to this work to heal my own wounds after a difficult time when I was young. What she helped me see was my counselling practice did not have to be this tough and that I didn't have to keep facing this beast from the past. Exploring what was going on was restorative and helped me to see that my self-care was important. I was suffering from compassion fatigue, and I was probably burning out doing that work. Without supervision I would not have realised this and I may have gone on to suffer depression and potentially I could have done harm to my clients by putting up personal defences against what I was hearing (see Godward, 2007).

Supervision as a place to be honest

Ideally your supervision session is a place where you can be honest and share your thoughts and concerns about your work. Where else will you do this?

Case study: Meera

Meera is a new trainee. She is working with a male client who expresses strong derogatory views about his female partner and shares some cruel controlling behaviour. Meera finds her client hard to like and sometimes switches off when he is speaking. She thinks he is deliberately trying to cause a reaction in her and she experiences him as controlling in the sessions.

Meera feels bad about not liking her client and feels like her work is poor. It is hard to admit that she doesn't always listen to him. Fortunately, she has good relationship with her supervisor and trusts them to not judge. She takes these thoughts and feelings to supervision and shares these difficulties. Her supervisor offers unconditional positive regard and helps Meera to explore these reactions. Even just voicing and sharing these feelings helps her to be more present with her client in the next session and gradually by listening more to him, she starts to understand why he behaves in this way. His own father had been a bully and he had learned to behave in this way. Through having a space with a non-judgemental counsellor, the client starts to regret his treatment of his partner and there is some hope for their relationship.

Meera continues to take this work to her supervisor to monitor what she is doing and her effectiveness and is making sure she can work with the client.

She also makes the link that she has been triggered by this client as he reminded her of an earlier relationship with a boyfriend who was mean to her. She realises that when she was shutting herself off, she had been protecting herself. Her supervisor gently suggests that this is an area to look at in personal therapy to enable her to be more effective with other such clients.

Here all the functions of supervision were required. The supervisor needed to monitor Meera's ethical practice and effectiveness as a therapist (normative).

There was some formative work where her supervisor had to help Meera learn how to bracket off her own thoughts and feelings and look at the importance of UPR in the relationship with this client. Finally, the restorative aspect was very important as Meera was reacting to client material, and this was affecting her ability to work effectively with him. She also needed to recognise the need for personal therapy.

I think it is important to work with a supervisor who isn't judging you or unduly assessing your practice. This is why having an external supervisor outside your placement agency can be a big advantage. Supervisors will still need to write reports on your progress and use of supervision for your training course but often this is done collaboratively rather than in a top-down assessing way. The supervisor's role is to monitor ethical practice and challenge you if you stray away from this, but it should be safe enough for you to share your misgivings, mistakes or difficulties otherwise it may become useless. E.g. What would happen if you only shared your successes and things you were pleased about with your supervisor?

Ponder points

What would stop you disclosing some of your work with clients?
What kind of things might you be reluctant to share?

There has been some interesting research into supervisee non-disclosure, particularly among trainees (see Mehr, Ladany and Caskie, 2010; Foskett and Van Vliet, 2021).

In the studies into this area the main points have been as follows:

- Feeling like the issue is too personal or involves overly negative feelings
- Worried about how the supervisor would see you
- See an issue as unimportant and irrelevant
- Don't want to be seen in a negative light or cause a negative reaction
- Feeling ashamed or embarrassed
- Worry that the supervisor may not be supportive
- Fear of looking incompetent

From the 2010 study and previous studies quoted in the article, there is a clear correlation shown between a positive relationship in supervision where there is a good working alliance and the ability for the trainee to disclose.

When we talk about a positive supervisory working alliance we are talking about 'the emotional bond between the supervisor and trainee and their agreement on the tasks and goals of supervision' (Mehr, Ladany and Caskie, 2010, p. 104).

This brings us to a look at what to do to prepare for supervision below.

How to prepare for effective supervision

Choosing a supervisor

This section will look at the importance of choosing an appropriate supervisor for you and how you prepare for your supervision sessions.

Supervisors differ greatly depending on their therapeutic background and approach. If you consider the three functions mentioned earlier some will veer more towards one function than another so you need to consider what you want in terms of these functions.

It might help to ask what you are looking for in your supervisor. Are you looking for:

- A *teacher* – someone to teach you how to counsel and work with your client
- A *confessor* – someone to share your thoughts and feelings and admit your mistakes
- A *dictator* – someone to tell you what to do and how to work
- A *parent* – someone to care for you during your training and support you/a safe base
- A *friend* – a confidante, person who gets on your level and who will support and not judge?

It might be interesting to rate these in order of importance for you. As all supervisees have different needs and preferences depending on personality and previous life experience and professional backgrounds.

There needs to be a good fit as this is an important and fairly long-term relationship, which you are embarking on. As tutors we normally recommend that you meet a few different people before deciding who to work with.

Sometimes students express dissatisfaction with their supervisors saying it is not challenging enough, or it is too challenging or they feel judged or they would like their supervisor to share more. Unless you state what you need, or negotiate this, your supervisor may not be aware of your needs or frustrations. Contracting for what you need in the first meeting may prevent this happening but as you grow as a therapist you may want something different. Supervisors are not mind readers and need to know if you are experiencing difficulties with them.

Supervisors can't always be what you want them to be.

Preparing for supervision sessions

To get the most from supervision, I would recommend taking some time to think what you want from each session. Remember it is your session and you will normally be setting the agenda.

It is useful to bring all your client work to supervision and review how things are going. You may have process notes that you can refer to when you go to supervision.

In between supervision session, it helps to keep a note of issues which arise in your counselling work. Some examples may be:

- Difficulties you are having with certain clients e.g., interpersonally
- Any themes occurring in your work with clients or generally

- Feeling unsure how to work with a client and how to approach the work
- Personal triggers which have come up for you in the counselling work
- Difficulties within your agency setting
- Ethical or legal issues you would like to discuss
- Course related issues

You may also take recordings or case studies to supervision provided that you have contracted with your clients to share their material in supervision. Most students make it clear that they are having supervision but also make it clear that they will not use real names.

It may be useful to make notes in your supervision and reflect on these sessions for your learning and development, as well as to help you with your coursework.

Bringing client cases to supervision: Using the super drone

As I have said, bringing your work to supervision is a lot more than just talking about the client's issues and how you are working. Hawkins and Shohet developed the Seven-Eyed Model of supervision in 1985 which looks at the different aspects of the counselling work and the supervision work, so that you and your supervisor can soar above the work you are doing and examine it from different angles like having a special drone. We will touch on it here, but see Hawkins and Shohet, (2012) for more information.

So what are the seven eyes? These are summarised below, and you can use these when thinking about your client and supervision.

1   The client: Focus here is on the client's issues and what they present and how they present in counselling.
2   The counselling work: This involves looking at your interventions and the way you work and the way you approach your work with clients.
3   The client-therapist relationship: It is really important to look at the quality of this. What are the dynamics between you and your client? How does the relationship feel?
4   The supervisee: Here the focus is on you, the therapist. What is happening for you consciously or unconsciously in this relationship with this client? This was shown particularly in the Jessie case study. Her personal factor, a history of abuse impacts on the way she is with the client and the way she sees him. How do you feel about your clients? Warm, cold, friendly? In supervision you will discover your implicit responses to clients. These are things which are outside of your awareness.
5   The supervisory relationship: Here it is worth considering the dynamics between you and your supervisor. What is the working alliance like? What is going on for you consciously when you go to supervision? Is there something that you don't understand which might indicate

unconscious factors. Often there is what is called a parallel process going on between you and them and you and your client. Simply put this is a situation which is playing out in supervision which is similar to one that plays out in your counselling relationship with the client e.g., you are desperate for your supervisor to tell you what to do just like your client is expecting you to tell them what to do (see Hawkins and Shohet, 2012 for a detailed look at this).

6 The supervisor's process: What is going on for your supervisor? It can be very useful when a supervisor shares their response to you and the material you are presenting. They may share their process and feelings. This may help shine a light on what is happening in the therapeutic relationship or may help expose hidden feelings or an unconscious process which is occurring. This can be vital in looking at an aspect of the work which has been missed. Some examples are given below:

- I feel under pressure to offer a solution to your problem with this client. Do you feel under pressure to offer them an answer when you are in your counselling session? (parallel process)
- When you were talking then I wanted to make things better for you as if you were a child. How are you seeing me? Like a mother? (possible transference and countertransference)
- Hearing the client's story and issues, I just felt really hopeless and sad. Is that how you are feeling about this now?

These are just examples of how your supervisor's honest impressions or sharing of feelings could help uncover what is going on in a relationship or allow for more exploration.

7 The wider context: Your client work and your supervision sessions do not take place in a vacuum. This eye focuses on the context in which you do your work and the societal impacts on what we do. This needs to be addressed in supervision as it impacts on what you can and can't offer your client and how you might feel about your work.

It is likely that in one session, you and your supervisee will use the different eyes to examine your practice and what else is going on. In the following example of a supervision session I have identified which eye our super drone was using.

The Seven Eyes in practice: A supervision session

Ethan came for a supervision session with me. I checked out how he was. He seemed a bit fed up.

He was feeling quite stuck with the client he was seeing. She did not seem to be making any progress and was bringing superficial things to talk about like her workplace and work friendships. She wasn't talking about the bigger issues she had originally come with (client).

I asked him what he was feeling when he was in the session with his client. He admitted that he sometimes felt a bit bored and sometimes switched off slightly. He wanted to move her on and encourage her to look at deeper things. He also wondered how someone in their mid-40s had not figured things out and stopped these damaging patterns by now (*supervisee*).

He reminded me that the client had come with issues around being in abusive and manipulative relationships. Everyone seemed to take advantage of her and her current partner was cruel and unkind. She had come wanting to look at how to manage her life and her relationships. Now she seemed to be just focussing on work (*client*).

This led to a discussion about women in society and the internalised values learned and the limits she had faced in terms of being working class with a poor education. She was still restricted in her choices due to being a single parent with three children in what she could do. This was useful as my supervisee recognised how inequality in society does impact (*context*).

We explored the counselling work he had been doing so far. He had been offering empathy and unconditional positive regard. It had been important that he had not passed any judgement about her lifestyle and choices in relationships. There were plenty of people in her life who did this and were vocal about what she should be doing. She also looked to others for approval, so he wanted to avoid being a person she had to please. This had helped her explore her situation and she had started to put down boundaries and had taken on the new job (*counselling work*).

Even though he was a male therapist working with a woman who may mistrust men, they had been able to build a relationship which had been positive, and she had felt able to share difficult aspects of her life. She looked forward to the sessions and felt she could breathe when she came. It was a space in a chaotic life (*client-counsellor relationship*).

At the beginning of the session, I recognised a need in me to find an answer to his stuckness and difficulty working with this client which was probably a parallel process with him wanting to help his client to move along. But I stepped back from this and as he explored his work, I was able to commend Ethan him on his approach and feel pleased with him that his client had made this progress. I wondered why he hadn't recognised this development in his client as being significant (*supervisor's process*).

He said that he had felt that he wasn't doing enough to help her. He had seen some similarities between himself and the client and the way she had been pushed around by significant others. He was expecting her to have a sudden 'light bulb' moment where it all became clear why she let people be dominant over her and this had not come. He was wondering if his approach, the person-centred one, was enough (*supervisee*).

We explored at this stage what counselling was about and that it wasn't about light bulbs and flashing lights usually, but could be quite a slog working with clients who had negative self-concepts which had built up and been reinforced over time (*counselling work*).

My process at this point was that I wondered if Ethan wanted to be some kind of saviour for his client. I have a bit of a revulsion to this as it smacks of guru-like qualities or being an expert, which rubs up against my values of creating equal, collaborative relationships (*supervisor's process*).

I asked him how he saw his client. He said she was like a ball of energy and that he thought she was a lovely person who was so kind to others but got kicked around by other people. He wished he could stop this. Just as he wished he could have been helped when he was bullied in the past. This led to a useful examination of how Ethan had been triggered by this client and a recognition that his role as a counsellor is not to rescue clients (*supervisee*).

We also looked at the Karpman's Drama triangle where a person can take on all the roles of victim, persecutor and rescuer at some stage. We recognised that the client presented like a victim and was persecuted by those around her, so it was natural that my supervisee had wanted to rescue her, but then was in danger of overdoing it and not actually helping her as a counsellor (for an accessible explanation of this, see Ballantine Dykes, Postings and Kopp, 2017) (*client-therapist relationship*).

By having a collaborative relationship which was based on trust and as free from judgement as possible, we were able to discuss what was going on for Ethan when he was working with the client and what might be going on for the client (*supervisory relationship*).

We discovered that the new job and good relationship with a colleague was a real step forward for the client and she was sharing this a lot because it meant that she was doing something positive in her life and that it was possible to have a good relationship with someone who was not manipulative and also, she was having fun (*client*).

As a result, Ethan was going to approach his work with more of an open mind and was going to really focus on what the client was saying about her work and her colleague and what this meant to her rather than remaining in his frame of reference with his agenda to change her life (*counselling work*).

From this you can see without our super drone with its seven eyes, there would not have been a full picture of what was going on in this work with the client.

The importance of feedback

In this example my supervisee was able to explore different aspects of his work but also could use me as a sounding board for what he had been doing and ask for feedback on some of his thoughts and feelings. I was able to affirm the work he was doing and also challenge him on some of his misunderstandings about counselling and his motives. If he had seemed like he wanted to be more of a friend to this person or more of a guru figure, I would have reflected this back to him as he would be blurring the counselling boundary.

It is important that you are able to ask for feedback from your supervisor and are able to take the feedback to be able to learn from supervision.

Ponder points

How are you at taking feedback?
What would you do if your supervisor challenged you about your practice?

Requirements for supervision: How much? How often?

It is important to be clear on how much supervision you need to meet the requirements of your course and the professional body which you have registered with as a trainee. These requirements will vary.

If you don't have enough hours of supervision to support your counselling work, you will not be able to count your client hours towards your training or accreditation later.

The amount of supervision you need also depends on how many client sessions you do per month, so it is important that you understand the ratios which your professional body and course have, so that you are properly supervised.

You also need to check how much in person supervision you need to have compared to remote face-to-face supervision.

Conclusion

In this chapter, I have looked at what supervision is and why it is important to you as a trainee counsellor or therapist. I have looked at the functions of supervision and how to prepare for your supervision both in terms of finding a suitable supervisor and also how to be ready for supervision session. An example from a supervision session was given and I highlighted the importance of feedback during supervision.

Finally, you were alerted to the need to ensure that you are having adequate supervision in line with your course and professional body requirements.

The overall aim was to prepare you for starting supervision and to help you get the most out of this. I hope this chapter has fulfilled this goal and you will find supervision an enriching experience as you develop as a practitioner.

References

Ballantine Dykes, F., Postings, T., and Kopp, B. (2017) *Counselling Skills and Studies.* London: Sage.

Karpman, S. (2014) *A Game Free Life.* Self published.

Foskett, A. J. and Van Vliet, K. J. (2021) Understanding supervisee non-disclosure in supervision with videorecording review and interpersonal process recall. *Counselling Psychotherapy Research*, 21, 188–197.

Godward, J. (2007) Cancerland. *Therapy Today*, 18(5), 18.

Hawkins, P. and Shohet, R. (2012) *Supervision in the Helping Professions.* Maidenhead: OU Press.

Henderson, P., Holloway, J., and Millar, A. (2014) *Practical Supervision.* London: JKP.

Inskipp, F. & Proctor, B. (2009) *The Art, Craft and Tasks of Supervision: Making the Most of Supervision.* London: Cascade.

Mehr, K., Ladany, N., and Caskie, G. (2010) Trainee non-disclosure in supervision: What are they not telling you? *Counselling and Psychotherapy Research*, 10(2), 103–113.

Chapter 15

The role of personal therapy in becoming a counsellor

Tara Fox

Introduction

This chapter explains the role of personal therapy in supporting you with the process of becoming a counsellor. You saw in Chapter 1 how courses are designed to raise awareness of your feelings and experiences of relating to others in the past and the present. This can feel overwhelming and although peer support may help you to get through some of the challenges of the trainee experience there will be some aspects of your life that are so private to you and therefore more safely taken to the care of a therapist. Anecdotal narratives of trainee counsellors are included to capture different experiences and to show how varied it can be for trainees in the therapy relationship. The perspective of the therapist is also considered when working with trainees as this role is different from working with other client groups.

In this chapter, I will help you to understand:

- the purpose of personal therapy during training
- how mandatory personal therapy during training can scaffold you through the expansion of self-awareness, growth, and skilfulness in the role of 'becoming a counsellor'
- the difference between counselling for personal growth as a trainee and counselling other client groups
- the key arguments in the personal therapy debate.

The purpose of personal therapy during training

Some courses require a minimum number of counselling sessions to help you with your self-awareness so that you can identify and confront any personal barriers and develop your capacity to work with vulnerable people. The intention of this requirement is to ensure that you have an opportunity to work through any issues from your past which may interfere with your ability to concentrate on the client's experience.

DOI: 10.4324/9781003405757-16

I remember worrying about the responsibility of the role of counsellor and questioning my ability to help clients. My experience of feeling responsible for other people's feelings was concerning me and I did not feel confident in myself. Counselling genuinely helped me to make sense of my anxiety. I was able to locate the origin of these worries and believe in the power of my natural warmth and the core conditions (Carkhuff, 1967) which I experience in relationships with others.

In a group exercise, I often ask students what they might need to bring to a counsellor. This initiates a dialogue between group members about what they carry with them each week including how it can feel overwhelming to manage their emotions on top of challenging assessments. Typically, groups mention feeling 'triggered' by the learning process itself. The topics and theories covered in class often resonate with students' life experiences and this can be unexpected and result in feelings of vulnerability and low self-esteem. Areas of life considered to be 'dealt with' can resurface in the light of new knowledge gained through training. Imposter syndrome (Clance and Imes, 1978) and self-doubt as well as problems with 'poor' work-life balance are also raised as concerns to be taken to therapy.

The strain of study can take its toll. Being observed in skills practice feels exposing and sharing personal stories about life experiences can feel intense and stir up material to be reflected upon in a journal and/or in therapy.

Psychological theory challenges you to self-reflect and this can feel energising but also anxiety-raising. You may experience pressure to confront your personal issues but not feel you are not ready (yet). Equally, you could have arrived on the course feeling a sense of questioning your life purpose and whether you can make your life more meaningful. These existential issues can be so overpowering and yet they reflect some of the issues clients may bring to you. A student might say:

> I feel like I am questioning everything at the moment. My marriage, my friendships, my parenting style and my desire to be on the course. This is the first time I have ever done something for me, my choice, my life, my contribution. I want to look back and know I have made a difference, and people might even remember me for something good.

Counselling for personal growth whilst in training

Peer support, tutor guidance and organisational support services combine to structure a positive learning opportunity, but counselling aims to ground you and keep you emotionally stable to embrace the peaks of insights and the lows of any preoccupied thoughts. Your personal development journal can capture your immediate concerns, but I would argue that the impactful nature of practitioner training needs the therapeutic input of a professional counsellor.

For many allowing themselves to be a client is tough. After all, you may have chosen this path to help others rather than yourself. Considering this it is likely that you may experience some resistance to the requirement and wonder why you should be forced to have personal therapy. The following shows how one Year 2 Diploma student felt. She reflects on her experience of mandatory therapy:

> On the morning of the first session, I noticed myself feeling a mixture of irritation and nervousness. I was annoyed that I was very busy, too busy to find time to have counselling and I had nothing that needed 'fixing' and didn't want to waste both our time. I especially didn't want to spend £50 on it.
>
> As there wasn't anything specific that I needed to bring to counselling, the first half of the session was speaking about my life now, I explained that things were going well and was leading a happy life, and then from out of the blue, I felt a wave of emotions sweep over me. I couldn't understand where it had come from, but it rocked me. It would be a few more sessions before I began to realise that I had been in a battle with myself for over 40 years.
>
> When I was twelve, I lost my mum to cancer and alongside that loss I also lost all the security and love from my world. We were left to be brought up by our father, who was very critical, unable to show emotions, had a short-temper and was frequently violent, especially towards me.
>
> Over the next few sessions, we gently unpicked my childhood and early adult life. I explored the impact those teenage years had on me. I slowly realised that, although I had physically left the situation behind decades earlier, my life had been impacted in every aspect. I had never felt safe, never learnt to truly trust anyone and had never thought I was good enough, clever enough, successful enough for anyone else, but more importantly I was not good enough for me.
>
> Counselling helped me realised that despite having a happy life now, one that I never could have imagined, I was not satisfied or happy because I could not stop striving to be better. I realise now that I was not seeking the feeling of being better, I was seeking the feeling of feeling safer. Counselling has been life-changing, it helped me realise I am safe.

The above shows how life-changing counselling during training can be, but also how this is perhaps not anticipated before starting, and there can be a reluctance to start especially if students have already had therapy previously.

Students who have engaged in counselling before may wonder why they can't count the hours they have done to meet the requirements. There are good reasons for this. Being in training demands you to know yourself better so that you can be self-aware of how you are coming across to others and how you experience other people. This personal development work may not have been the focus of the work you have undertaken in therapy previously.

Your 'task' as a client in training has a purpose: for you to feel more resilient to hearing and being with other people's life stories which may be traumatic and deeply upsetting. Should your story be similar to the client's story then this can trigger your emotions and distract you from concentrating and experiencing the client's narrative with them. It could also prevent you from working at depth on their issues.

Chapter 8 speaks about the experiential group and explains how you can get in touch with powerful memories and strong feelings from interacting with other students, your peers. These encounters can start to build up in your mind and you will benefit from taking your feelings and thoughts about all of this to a personal therapist. There may be parts of your life you feel you have already worked through and come to terms with and suddenly these seem to be not quite so resolved as you thought they were. Equally, there may be a worry about uncovering new things you weren't aware of. I recommend if your course allows you some choice, you decide to start therapy when it suits you the best so there is some space around you to seek comfort, take care of yourself and rest. Starting sooner may help you to be more effective in your therapeutic work, so avoid leaving it until the end when it can't support you through the training journey. Counselling can also help you understand theory too which can improve your capacity to support your clients.

The following case study explains how Afi (pseudonym) experienced this and how it was possible to learn from Tonkin's model of grief (Tonkin, 1996) theory in the counselling room.

Case study: Afi

I realised I had so many losses that were preventing me from being able to support others through their grief. At first, I thought I could avoid it, but I realised that loss is a part of life, and all clients would end up talking about it in some way. I could not avoid it in skills practice too and I felt anxious about keeping it all together. I couldn't handle looking at this while I had all the assignments to do so I waited until the summer when I felt safe enough to talk about it without the pressure of needing to think and research for essays. I had counselling weekly and began to open up about my fears of sadness and grief. I was worried these feelings would overwhelm me, but the kindness of the therapist and her safe space meant I could trust her with my vulnerabilities. We spoke about the models of loss and grief including the Tonkin's model. I realised I could grow around my grief and some days I would be sadder than others. I made a place in the garden to be with my loved ones to keep in touch with them. This was really emotional, but I had to face up to it.

- What do you notice about Afi's decision to do this therapeutic work?
- How do you imagine this work will help Afi with client work?
- Is there anything else you think Afi needs to be mindful of?

A study by Edwards (2018) found that counselling students in therapy enhanced their learning about the therapeutic role when attending therapy 'beyond the textbook' illustrating how the experience of being a client leads to deeper emotional learning and greater insight.

The counselling trainee as client

Therapists who offer their services to trainees have a special lens on the client through their unique position of the counsellor/psychotherapist and experience of being the trainee. Not all therapists choose to do this work. What is the difference between counselling for personal growth in training and counselling other client groups? I asked two experienced therapists the following questions:

1   Are there any special considerations you must attend to when working with trainees as opposed to other client groups?
2   What are your thoughts about this?

Here are a couple of responses from two experienced practitioners who offer this work:

THERAPIST 1
Question 1: The main considerations are to ensure that I understand that trainee counsellors initially come with a purpose to find and address issues which may influence their practice. Then together we can begin to explore what they need for themselves to aid resilience and improved emotional stability and have increased self-awareness and they know themselves enough to prevent overidentification with clients and reduce the possibility of secondary trauma. I am not working with their client and yet ultimately this will improve their experience of counselling with a trainee.

Question 2: Trainees can be resistant to having personal therapy as they have so many demands on their time and energy. It is often difficult to gain an initial commitment to personal exploration and discovery. Where a person has undertaken limited self-development, they may also come with a need to theorise their issues rather than to engage with in-depth therapeutic work. This may lead to trainees feeling frustrated and ultimately a rupture in the therapeutic relationship. However, where a trainee is committed to gaining personal insight and experiencing opportunities to grow it can be amongst the most rewarding aspects of work as this improves and enhances the whole profession.

THERAPIST 2
Question 1: It is important that trainees prepare before accessing counselling. Personal counselling during training offers an opportunity to develop self-awareness, process personal material and as a space to

develop as a practitioner. I have supported trainees to consider goal set-ting to help focus their counselling and training. We may begin by clar-ifying what counselling is, and how it can work. Undergoing counselling can be challenging, it can provide clear insight into what our clients may experience. This can include feeling anxious at the start (and/or during) counselling, feeling more emotional than usual, and noticing changes you begin to instigate in your life through counselling. It also provides us with the opportunity to create/develop awareness of our own triggers/blind spots/judgements/unconscious biases. This allows us to become more self-aware counsellors.

Question 2: I have come across trainees who approach personal coun-selling merely as a requirement of their course and don't want to engage fully in the process. This can provide a real challenge, and I do not feel able to work with trainees who turn up but do not show up as themselves. Personal counselling is similar to supervision in that it requires prepara-tion, readiness and openness for change. Trainees who fully engage in their counselling can find it may instigate further self-reflection through journaling or specific assignments that require a view of how this skill is developing.

These views show how important it is to prepare for being a client and how personal therapy is certainly not a tick-box exercise but a central component of the course that needs as much attention as other parts of the training process. The significance of therapy in these anecdotes implies a link between student success on the course and counsellor competence when working with clients. I prompted the above therapists to explain their views of how a trainee therapist-client differs from other client groups. They offered the following advice:

THERAPIST 1: It is important for students to attend a therapist modelling their chosen modality as this can give a real insight into the client experience and thereby improve empathic depth in their own practice. There is the opportunity to see how theory and skills are linked too through the way the counsellor shows how their experience informs the interventions. It can increase understanding of the rhythm of therapy undertaken within specific perspectives.

THERAPIST 2: As a counsellor, I focus on creating conditions for the trainee to relax and trust the space, and for it to be a learning opportunity. This includes providing additional psycho-education and deeper discussion than I would for other client groups. We may explore specific theories or ways of working relevant to the trainee and their course. The trainee may want to explore the impact of particular parts of the training course on them, i.e., experientials, skills or how they relate to individuals on the course. This is helpful content to bring to sessions if the trainee is strug-gling to know what to talk about.

These experiences show how professionals have respect and empathy for trainees and work hard to create an environment of safety for them as the student and client.

These examples also show how switching between being a client who is focused on your own process to attending to the counsellor's process may feel untherapeutic. Furthermore, because you are likely to keep an eye on the counsellor's interventions and how they respond to you there is a dual positionality of 'client' and 'trainee counsellor' occurring within you. This can be therapeutic when your counsellor is transparent about their process and commitment to helping you to heal but if the relationship does not feel safe then these congruent encounters will feel more difficult to respond to.

Poor experiences of therapy

We know from research that it is the relationship that counts, the development of a 'therapeutic alliance' (Norcross, 2002; Cooper, 2008) when it comes to the success of therapy. Sometimes students have difficult experiences in therapy but may feel like they must stay with it. It is important to bring your concerns about the counsellor to your supervisor and or personal development group to work out what may be at play in the interaction. Often the payoff from confronting your feelings with the counsellor is productive, allowing you to have meaningful communication. This has been called 'a rupture' in counselling and is highly valued for its opportunity to improve the therapeutic nature of the relationship. At other times the relationship is not the best fit for you both. In a nutshell, I recommend speaking with the counsellor to see if you can make it work first. Then if this doesn't work swap to a new counsellor rather than pushing on through and counting the hours. One of the negatives Edwards found in her 2018 literature review was a lack of support from courses that didn't help when students were facing any difficulties in therapy. She concludes that trainees need clear written guidance to follow in order to empower themselves.

Review the activity below to prepare you for the therapy component of your training. This should help you to firm up some ideas about what your counselling could be like.

Activity

Consider how you feel about going to see a counsellor:

- How are you feeling about starting personal therapy?
- What sort of a counsellor would you want?
- Draw them or sketch a few words to describe them.
- What would they help you to do?
- What difference would that make to you in your life?

Key arguments in the debate

Although the British Association for Counselling and Psychotherapy (BACP) does not specify that trainees need to have personal therapy during training over 50% of their accredited courses include this requirement (McMahon, 2018). The British Psychological Society's division of counselling psychology require a mandatory requirement of 40 hours of personal therapy as a minimum for trainees in recognition of the significance of the relationship and the therapist's use of self in clinical work. (Rizq and Target, 2008). The pros and cons of therapy are presented below.

Table 15.1 Overview of the debates about personal therapy in training

For therapy	Against therapy
Tutor experiences support the value the role of therapy in training.	Mandatory therapy does not guarantee self-development
Student experiences report how this is important and needed	Little research evidence to show mandatory therapy is of benefit or that it equals being a better therapist (Chaturvedi, 2013)
Useful to know what it feels like to be a vulnerable client including experiencing emotions and endings	Experiencing vulnerability as a client does not necessarily increase empathy for the client's vulnerability
Students can use their therapist as a role model (Rizq and Target, 2008) to help them to observe and experience a professional counsellor at work	Students can observe tutors in demos to see skills in action.
Increasing self-awareness by looking at how past events, and relationships have impacted can prevent harm to clients (prejudices, biases, over identifying with client problems)	If students are watching how the therapist works, then they are not emersed in the process of their own therapy.
During therapy students realise they have unfinished business or unresolved issues.	Trainees who are not ready to go into therapy may be wasting their time and money.
Therapy helps trainees recognise 'wounded healer' traits such as the need to rescue others in unhealthy ways such as colluding with clients' unhelpful patterns of behaviour.	People who don't want therapy don't use it properly and not everyone who wants to be a therapist is a 'wounded healer.'
Students who are open to personal development need support for this work.	Some students are angry about being forced into therapy so disengage.
Having counselling can increase confidence and self-esteem.	Many other aspects of training can contribute to this development including class activities, role plays etc

For therapy	Against therapy
Personal therapy is a big support for issues that arise in the Personal Development (PD) group, providing a private space.	Students' personal development can be supported in other ways such as the PD group and supervision.
The need for therapy means students are given the chance to increase emotional literacy rather than being defensive.	Therapists may feel conflicted taking money from a client who does not want to be there, and it can be hard working with clients who do not wish to be there.

Source: Adapted from Dale, Godward and Smith, 2020, pp. 129–137

Ponder points

Given the choice and cost of therapy, it is possible students would not self-refer to counselling, without the course requirement being a motivator.
What are your thoughts on this debate?

Conclusion

This chapter has explored the purpose of personal therapy during training. It has stressed how more than peer support is needed for the expansion of your self-awareness.

It is beneficial for you to work on any issues from your past and present life that may get in the way of 'being there' for clients. Allowing yourself to be a client can help you to work delicately with other people's vulnerabilities and move you towards self-compassionate responses to the inevitable challenge of psychotherapeutic work.

References

Carkhuff, R. R. (1967) *Helping and Human Relations Volume 1: Selection and Training.* New York: Holt, Rinehart and Winston.

Chaturvedi, S. (2013) Mandatory personal therapy: does the evidence justify the practice? In debate. *British Journal of Guidance and Counselling*, 41, 454–460.

Clance, P. R. and Imes, S. A. (1978) The imposter phenomenon in high achieving women: dynamics and therapeutic intervention. *Psychotherapy, Theory, Research and Practice*, 15(3), 241–247.

Cooper, M. (2008) *Essential Research Findings in Counselling and Psychotherapy: The Facts are Friendly.* London: Sage.

Dale, H., Godward, J., and Smith, C. (2019) Personal therapy in counsellor training. In Godward, J., Dale, H., and Smith, C. (Eds), *Personal Development Groups for Trainee Counsellors: An Essential Companion* (pp. 129–137). Oxford: Routledge.

Edwards, J. (2018) Counseling and psychology student experiences of personal therapy: A critical interpretive synthesis. *Frontiers in Psychology*, 9, 1732.

McMahon, A. (2018) Irish clinical and counselling psychologists' experiences and views of mandatory personal therapy during training: A polarisation of ethical concerns. *Clinical Psychology and Psychotherapy*, 25(3), 415–426.

Norcross, J. C. (Ed.) (2002) *Psychotherapy Relationships that Work: Therapist Contributions and Responsiveness to Patients.* Oxford University Press.

Rizq, R. and Target, M. (2008) "Not a little Mickey Mouse thing": How experienced counselling psychologists describe the significance of personal therapy in clinical practice and training. Some results from an interpretative phenomenological analysis. *Counselling Psychology Quarterly*, 21, 29–48.

Tonkin, L. (1996) TTC, Cert Counselling (NZ) Growing around grief: Another way of looking at grief and recovery. *Bereavement Care*, 15(1), 10.

Conclusion

Where are you now?

Jayne Godward and Tara Fox

This book has taken you through the transformative process of becoming a counsellor. We have presented a transparent overview of the pathway from first steps to qualifying as a counsellor showing you an insider's perspective to support you along the journey.

In Chapter 1, we looked at what is involved in counselling and psychotherapy training and the teaching and learning methods involved. Therapy training works with your head, heart and mind meaning you are in it!

Chapter 2 really looked at why people choose to become therapists and encouraged you to look at your hidden motivations for choosing this career path.

In Chapter 3, we helped you to understand the recruitment and selection procedure to prepare you for the application process.

Chapter 4 raised awareness of the challenges and struggles you may face as you look at yourself during the personal development work on the course including unconscious aspects. This will help you prepare for the personal demands of your training.

Chapter 5 gave you different activities to increase your knowledge of multiple identities in yourself and in others. It helped you to consider how the course experience will prepare you for working with difference in client work.

Chapter 6 examined how undertaking counselling training can affect the person's relationships, in particular, that with their spouse or partner and looked at ways this can be navigated. The information presented about the impact on self and others helps you to choose the best time to train as a therapist from a more informed position.

An overview of the main theoretical models underpinning counselling and psychotherapy qualifications was given in Chapter 7. This included Person-Centred, Psychodynamic, Integrative and Relational approaches. Activities prompted consideration of the main factors to consider when choosing a training programme.

Chapter 8 highlighted the importance of relational connection in becoming a counsellor by looking at the importance of the group experience, including the personal development group and the course group.

DOI: 10.4324/9781003405757-17

In Chapter 9, we explored the 'shift' in becoming a counsellor, a movement or transformation in the self, which is important, particularly for working relationally with others. Three recent trainees shared their experiences to demonstrate this.

Chapter 10 attended to resilient behaviours and humility, examining ways to reframe difficulties as opportunities for growth in the face of adversity. Typical barriers to development are explained to normalise different reactions to the expectations of counselling training.

Chapter 11 attended to the preparation for placement including the significance of the first client experience. It gave a flavour of what starting work with clients involves and an understanding of the demands of working therapeutically with others.

In Chapter 12, we examined the impact that our society and the world we live in has particularly on clients, but also on their counsellors. We looked at some important issues which come into the counselling room, and it was suggested that client symptoms and anxiety are often the product of their environments rather than an individual problem.

Chapter 13 considered self-kindness, self-compassion, and community thus reframing self-care as a compassionate activity essential for working in the service of others. It included findings from new research with 53 trainee therapists which shows many ways to restore and replenish the self-whilst working with clients 'soul to soul'.

The value of supervision and what it involves were discussed in Chapter 14. We looked at the functions of supervision and how to approach this activity, so that you can get the most out of the opportunity that this special relationship provides during your training and beyond.

Finally, Chapter 15 discussed the role of personal therapy from the perspective of both the trainee and the counsellor who is working with the trainee as this role is different from working with other client groups. The key arguments in the personal therapy debate were presented and discussed and anecdotal narratives of trainee counsellors are included.

We hope that this book has supported you in your steps towards becoming a counsellor or psychotherapist and will continue to be a useful resource for you as you progress through your training.

Index

For Product Safety Concerns and Information please contact our EU
representative GPSR@taylorandfrancis.com
Taylor & Francis Verlag GmbH, Kaufingerstraße 24, 80331 München, Germany